The New York Times

WILL SHORTZ'S
FAVORITE CROSSWORD PUZZLES

Edited by Will Shortz

ST. MARTIN'S GRIFFIN ❦ NEW YORK

ISBN 0-312-30613-X

First Edition: October 2002

10 9 8 7 6 5 4 3 2 1

INTRODUCTION

As someone whose favorite movie of the year is rarely, if ever, named best picture, whose favorite TV show is never number one on the Nielsens, and who hardly ever does anything fashionable, I feel a little uncomfortable picking 75 "favorite" crosswords for this book.

Still, someone has to make the choices, and I have the advantage of having been an enthusiastic solver (as well as puzzlemaker) since about age 8. My first puzzle was published when I was 14. I sold my first crossword to The New York Times at age 22; the year was 1975, during the era of Will Weng, The Times's second crossword editor. And since I succeeded Eugene T. Maleska to become only the fourth crossword editor in the newspaper's history, I've kept close tabs on solvers' reactions to the puzzles.

What's hard? What's easy? What's enjoyable, and what's not? What excites you, what annoys you, and what leaves you wondering "huh"?

Letters, phone calls and e-mails pour into my office, giving me an immediate impression of solvers' opinions. I read The New York Times's online crossword forum several times a day, giving me even faster feedback. I also attend puzzle-related events throughout the year. Perhaps best of all, every Times crossword is tested by four veteran solvers before publication (in time for me to do last-minute polishing), so comments about the puzzles from a trusted panel arrive even before the puzzles see print.

This volume contains my 75 favorite daily New York Times crosswords since 1993, when I assumed the editorship. They represent what are in my opinion the best of the best, chosen based on my own feelings as well as comments from solvers.

What makes them special?

For starters, every Times crossword has to follow some basic rules—applicable to almost all American crosswords—to be even considered for publication:

- The pattern of black-and-white squares must be symmetrical
- Unkeyed letters (that is, ones that appear in only one answer) are taboo
- Two-letter words are taboo, too
- All words must be in good taste
- The grid must have allover interlock—which means that the black squares may not cut the grid into separate pieces
- The grid can't have too many black squares
- Words can't be repeated
- Every answer must have a printed reference or else be in common use in everyday speech or writing

Constructing a crossword under such constraints isn't easy, as anyone who has ever tried will attest. But meeting these standards is enough only to get the work considered. I receive eight to ten submissions for every puzzle that is accepted for publication, so an accepted puzzle must go beyond the minimum standards.

For a puzzle to be accepted, I look for a fresh, interesting, narrowly defined theme (assuming there is a theme), accessible to everyone and consistently applied throughout; lively, colorful vocabulary; and a minimum of obscurity and crosswordese. The grid must be 15 x 15 squares. The maximum number of entries allowed is 78 (or 72, if the puzzle is unthemed).

Beyond the above, I enjoy puzzles with humor. I like unusual letter patterns and words containing the rarer letters of the alphabet, like J, Q, X and Z. I encourage phrases from everyday writing and speech, whether or not they're in a dictionary, because they tend to have pizzazz, and they're less likely to have appeared in puzzles before. An excess of proper names is discouraged, because people tend either to know them or not—and if a puzzle has a spot with several tough names, it's easy for a solver to get stuck. The quality of the contributor's clues doesn't matter to the same degree, because I know, as editor, I can change them if necessary. On average about half the clues in The Times's crosswords are my own.

In my first 8½ years on the job, which is the period covered in this book, I've edited more than 2,600 daily puzzles for The Times—from which these 75 were selected. They are presented in chronological order.

What makes each of the puzzles special enough to be called a "favorite" is explained at the top of its page. At the bottom of the page are the author's name and the date and the day of the week of original publication in The Times. As you may know, the crosswords in The Times get more difficult as the week proceeds, from Monday (easy) to Saturday (very hard), so noting the day of the week before you begin will help you gauge the puzzle's difficulty.

My favorite puzzles tend to have more gimmickry than the puzzles in The Times as a whole. Unusual twists stand out. Often these are the puzzles that people remember and talk about. I'm not sure you'd want a steady diet of gimmickry; for everyday solving, traditional puzzles can bring just as much pleasure. But a book of favorites has its own rules.

The ages of the puzzle constructors vary from teens to 70's. In a few cases, the only puzzle a constructor ever had in the newspaper appears here. At the other extreme, some of The Times's most frequent and popular puzzle contributors do not appear in the book at all, because their work is of a quieter, less flashy sort. Their absence doesn't mean they're any less valued.

A word about computers: Nowadays many solvers may assume that crosswords are created by computer. This is not true for the crosswords in The Times. While it's true that computer assistance is being increasingly used by constructors for suggesting possible entries or fills for areas of a grid, a computer can't say what is a good word or an interesting fill. Only a human can make that judgment.

Moreover, a computer program to construct crosswords is only as good as the database it comes with. And the English language is so vast, with so many idioms and phrases and names from the world around us, reference works can't begin to include them all. Some constructors who use computer assistance have spent years supplementing their databases with fresh, colorful names and phrases not found in any references. In a sense, the computer has become an extension of each constructor's personality.

Beyond the grid, only a human can think of an original puzzle theme or write an original clue. And I painstakingly continue to edit every puzzle by hand, clue by clue, on paper, the old-fashioned way.

Thus, when you tackle a New York Times crossword, rest assured that you're still pitting your mind against another mind, not a machine.

Herewith 75 of the best crosswords that the human mind can produce!

—Will Shortz, 2002

SHORTZ SAYS:
The first weekday crossword that I edited for The New York Times has a simple theme, familiar vocabulary and mostly straightforward clues—suitable for the easiest puzzle of the week. Simple doesn't mean bland, though. Note, for example, the colorful answer at 33-Across, which is not the sort of pop-cultural phrase found often in older puzzles.

ACROSS

1 Understood
4 Some tracks
9 __ Rizzo ('69 Hoffman role)
14 Santa __ winds
15 Actress Anouk
16 Significant person?
17 Kauai keepsake
18 Small person
20 Legit
22 Caroline Schlossberg, to Ted Kennedy
23 Type style: Abbr.
24 Big Mama
25 Church part
29 Rummy variety
32 The mark on the C in Čapek
33 Calendar period, to Kirk
37 Caustic substance
38 Traditional tune
40 Pub quaff
42 Logical newsman?
43 Long-lasting curls
45 Depicts
49 Health-food store staple
50 Jerry Herman composition
53 Dash
54 Michelangelo masterpiece
56 Journalist Greeley
58 Used booster cables
62 Tina's ex
63 Correspond, grammatically
64 Regarded favorably
65 Pince-__
66 Former Justice Byron
67 Air-show maneuvers
68 Palindrome center

DOWN

1 French
2 __ time (singly)
3 Taipei's land
4 Honolulu locale
5 Fat fiddle
6 Fuse word
7 First name in hotels
8 Big rigs
9 Campus mil. grp.
10 Daughter of Zeus
11 Calendar abbr.
12 Theology sch.
13 Eye
19 __-man (flunky)
21 Hooch container
24 Magna __
26 Rights grp.
27 "Oy __!"
28 __ out (supplement)
30 Hoosegows
31 Footrace terminus
32 Stage actress Hayes
34 MS follower?
35 Love, Italian style
36 Newcastle-upon- __, England
38 Esne
39 Judge's exhortation
40 Prone
41 Name of 13 popes
44 Oscar the Grouch, for one
46 Julia Louis-Dreyfus on "Seinfeld"
47 Pool-ball gatherer
48 Common cause for blessing
50 Strawberry, once
51 "Any Time __" (Beatles tune)
52 Auto-racer Andretti
55 Words of comprehension
56 "David Copperfield" character
57 Ten to one, e.g.
58 Gossip
59 "That's disgusting!"
60 High-tech med. diagnostics
61 Foreman stat

by Fred Piscop   Monday, November 22, 1993

2

SHORTZ SAYS:
This puzzle caused quite a stir when it was published, because its thematic "trick" was still fairly novel at the time. As with all the puzzles in this book, I'd rather not reveal the twist before you solve . . . but I think you'll enjoy it when you get it!

ACROSS

1 Privy
5 U.S. narc
9 Egg depository
13 Clear (out)
14 Sum up
16 "__ any wonder?"
17 Thompson of films
18 "You __ Beautiful"
19 The Coasters' record label
20 Wow everyone
23 Self-defense item
24 Mer material
25 "I Fall to Pieces" singer
27 Trash pickup spot
32 Greenspan and Paton
33 Super-growth locales
34 __ sequitur
35 Summoned, in a way
36 Jockey rival
37 Transceiver button
38 Prefix with literal or lateral
39 Does a laundry job
40 Party you can't crash
41 Family assets
43 Dance movement
44 Fearful cry
45 Enfant terrible
46 John Guare play, with "The"
52 Via Veneto farewell
53 St. __ (London site)
54 Amusement park staple
57 Trade grp.
58 Frontier trophy
59 Eye part
60 Henri's head
61 Orange and lemon, e.g.
62 Gatsby portrayer, 1949

DOWN

1 Uncover, poetically
2 Site of a Napoleon victory, 1805
3 Pyramid, perhaps
4 Moving tribute?
5 Daze
6 Road sign
7 Handled perfectly
8 Publius Ovidius __
9 Break
10 O.T. book
11 Decorous
12 Kind of search
15 Juggernauts
21 McKellen and Fleming
22 Catches
25 Santa __, Calif.
26 Music man Lester
27 Short story
28 Salt Lake City team
29 "Baby, __ Your Loving"
30 "Twicknam Garden" poet
31 Christie's "Peril at __"
32 Specialized movie theater
33 Detriment
36 Circuits
37 Nasty
39 Cartoonist Silverstein
40 Olympic skater Johann __ Koss
42 Filet
43 Perceives
45 Debutante
46 Pest controller of a sort
47 French flower
48 Express
49 Per
50 Outdoor feast
51 Fiji's capital
55 Nancy Drew's beau
56 Self-promotional notice in a magazine

by Chet Currier

Friday, May 27, 1994

SHORTZ SAYS:

The hidden theme of this puzzle is revealed at 21-Across, so if you'd like to delay the surprise as long as possible, wait to solve this part of the grid until the end. Besides the theme, note the lively answers at 7- and 52-Across, and 3-, 11-, 19-, 30-, 40- and 48-Down. That's expert puzzle-making!

3

ACROSS

1 Apple competitor
4 Gambler Holliday
7 Fifth-century pope
12 Green
14 The "S" in T. S. Eliot
16 Men of La Mancha
17 Farmer's tipcart
18 Cartridge type
19 Aviatrix, for short
20 Point of no return?
21 Hidden theme of this puzzle
24 Last word of "Finnegans Wake"
25 Make an appeal
26 White House monogram
27 Outfit
29 Make an appeal
30 Miners' sch.
32 Out of sorts
33 Friend of 21-Across
35 Affected by pollen
38 "Clan of the Cave Bear" heroine
39 Chosen number?
42 Anwar's successor
43 Pickpocket
44 Slangy hello
45 New York eng. sch.
46 Like 33-Across's apple
50 Suffix meaning "small one"
51 Pack animal?
52 Laid-back
53 Quick to blush
56 London barrister
58 Game officials
59 Making out
60 Hot time in Chile
61 Umpteen's ordinal?
62 Green lights

DOWN

1 Hosp. hookups
2 Doctors often carry them

3 Franciscus TV drama of the 60's
4 "Dream Lover" singer
5 With no letup
6 Price abbr.
7 Material
8 Pro follower
9 Dog, for short
10 Proof goof
11 Minimal ante
13 A bit obtuse
14 Maze word
15 Droopy-eyed
19 Corset result, perhaps
21 Where fat cats get thin

22 "I'm glad that's over!"
23 Sealy rival
28 N.H.-Vt. neighbor
30 Open
31 Whirligig
32 Actor Gerard
33 Boxer's title, briefly
34 Short shot?
35 Daphne and hazel
36 It's like home?
37 Bomber Boomer
39 Beethoven's only opera
40 Sight saver?
41 Peaked
43 Cockpit display
44 Mrs. Rockefeller

47 Former capital of Bolivia
48 Underground event
49 __ gland
54 It ended in 1806: Abbr.
55 Two or go follower
56 X
57 Football linemen: Abbr.

by Bob Klahn

Friday, September 9, 1994

4

SHORTZ SAYS:
The 11 capitalized Across clues in this puzzle reveal its unusual theme. As a rule, the theme answers in a crossword are arranged in symmetrical positions in the grid, but here some extras have been squeezed in where they will fit, adding more pleasure to the solving.

ACROSS

1 COPPER CHARGES
8 MERCURY WATER SOURCES
15 Furniture piece
16 Glee
17 Competitor
18 "O, where is __?": Shakespeare
19 Hemingway novel setting
20 Bygone auto
21 Quarantine
22 Ship officers
24 Of oneself: Lat.
25 GOLDEN GALE
28 POTASSIUM PORTIONS
33 TIN SOURCE
34 HYDROGEN GAS
35 Auction offering
36 Mauritanian, e.g.
37 Like Oscar Wilde
38 Flintstone pet
39 Zip
40 Imagine that!
41 CARBON COOKER
42 SILVER DEBRIS
45 NEON PORTAL
46 O.T. book
47 Recreational drives
49 Grants
53 Take measures
54 Boz boy
57 Lets, in tennis
58 Bug River locale
60 Current instrument
61 Some new-car drivers
62 HELIUM DRINKS
63 ALUMINUM FISHING GEAR

DOWN

1 Mediocre marks
2 The __ Reader (alternative press magazine)
3 Pro __
4 Cabinet dept.
5 Scented blossom
6 He went to camp in a 1987 movie
7 __ Hall
8 Port opening
9 Back-of-the-book section
10 Rad
11 Latin list extender
12 Actress Kedrova
13 Senator from Mississippi
14 Backwater
22 Bedroom community, for short
23 Kerrigan and company
25 Yoga position
26 Take apart
27 Strive mightily, with "out"
29 U.S. poet laureate __ Dove
30 Former Twin batting champ
31 Largish singing group
32 Attack in a way
34 Bury
37 Recalled
38 Follows hostilely
41 Indispensable
43 __ one's head
44 Slightly tapered
45 Monticello site
48 Comic Poundstone
49 Esau's wife
50 Approach
51 Search
52 Lith. and Lat., once
54 Deck
55 Memo words
56 Dining hall
59 Tempe sch.

by Randolph Ross   Friday, September 16, 1994

SHORTZ SAYS:
The reason for the extra square at the top of this puzzle will become evident once you solve 1-Down. Three other answers provide hints to the theme. Note the date that this puzzle first appeared.

ACROSS

2 Links org.
5 Hollers
10 Support
14 Speech fumbles
15 Charlotte cager
16 Mitch Miller's instrument
17 Bandleader Edmundo
18 Mr. Kosygin
19 "Lean __" (Bill Withers hit)
20 The Smothers Brothers, e.g.
21 Alice's restaurant
22 Make hand over fist
24 Open
26 Bottom-line amount
28 "Odyssey" enchantress
29 Antic
30 Chopin's "Butterfly" et al.
32 February 2 sighting
34 Brighton brew
35 Carved out
39 Cauldron
40 Like a certain period of burrowed time?
43 Singer Christie
44 Consent and Reason, e.g.
46 "Six Crises" monogram
47 37-Down, e.g.
49 They're on the receiving end
52 Cross
53 Maid-for-TV?
56 "Steve Allen Show" regular
57 "Romancero gitano" poet
59 Handsome hunk
61 Cowboys and Indians, e.g.
63 Physicist Georg
64 Actress Diana
65 Casual coverup

67 Stock option
68 Clairvaux cleric
69 Elizabeth I, to poets
70 System start-up
71 Salt deposit?
72 Hornless, as cattle
73 "Citizen Kane" studio

DOWN

1 For the outlook, look out for his look out!
2 Lost in Lille
3 What 1-Down is
4 Hobnob
5 Shock treatments?
6 Pit
7 Blackmailer's words

8 Driver's aid
9 Be up and about
10 Fond of reading
11 Dogpatch denizen
12 "Cathy," e.g.
13 Nancy Drew's creator
23 Virtuoso
25 Postfix
27 Slipper
31 Adjudge
32 Toning-up spot
33 In fighting trim
36 George Gallup competitor
37 What 3-Down is
38 Ding-a-ling
41 Mutant cartoon superheroes

42 Site of 1905's Norway-Sweden split
45 "The Faerie Queene" poet
48 "Who Slew Auntie __?" (1971 film)
50 Bard of boxing
51 Any soap opera
53 Set upon
54 Kind of brick
55 Kazantzakis character
58 "Are not!" response
60 What to do when you see red
62 D-Day river
66 Letters angels love?

by Bob and Sharon Klahn   Thursday, February 2, 1995

6

SHORTZ SAYS:
Sometimes simple is best, even wonderful, as this puzzle's theme proves—especially when all the elements of it are included. This was the constructor's first published crossword anywhere. What a debut!

ACROSS

1 Fantastik competitor
7 Minimum
12 60's space project
13 Polyester sheets
15 Show horse
16 Trident carrier
18 Jewel
19 "__ Rhythm"
21 Riyadh residents
22 Blitzed
24 TV's "Tales from the __"
25 Weaselly animal
28 Boston airport
30 Doe follower, in song
31 Botticelli subject
32 Lawyers' org.
35 Budget item
36 Fits (inside)
37 Kind of history
38 Compass heading
39 Aligns, temporally
40 Bring forth
41 Disney dog
42 Father of the Titans
43 50's White House name
46 Tap type
48 One of nine
50 Results
51 Warning to Bo-Peep
54 Buckle up
56 Offering a neologism
58 Meaning
59 A Mouseketeer
60 Ground
61 Nullify

DOWN

1 Parisian head
2 Utah city
3 Street drug
4 Florida city
5 Eugene's place
6 "The Prisoner of Chillon" poet
7 K-O string
8 Potato buds
9 Guanaco relatives
10 General Motors product
11 Hubert's wife, in the comics
12 Food additive
14 Trim a tress
17 Superlative suffix
20 Means of spotting this puzzle's theme?
22 Editor's notation
23 Some pieces of advice
25 Damages
26 Summer beverages
27 Artist Magritte
29 Astronaut Grissom
31 Relieves
32 Elvis's middle name
33 Capital on the Caspian
34 XXX drinks
36 Big Apple sch.
37 Ellipsoid
39 Train car
40 Causing to disappear
41 Mexican festival feature
42 Ruined
43 Brit. legislators
44 Prefix with meter
45 1918 battle site
47 Like some pre-Columbian art
49 Hue
51 Ship post
52 Part of A.M.
53 Point in life
55 Advanced degree?
57 Teachers' grp.

by Jeremy Thomas Paine   Wednesday, May 10, 1995

SHORTZ SAYS:
In this high-wire act of puzzle-making, the letter I is the clue for 19- and 53-Across, the black squares in the middle of the grid form a large capital I . . . and every clue begins with I as well!

ACROSS

1 Ingemar Johansson wins
4 Inhabitant's place
9 Industrialist's deg.
12 Insurance figure
14 Ichthyologist's specimen
15 "It's Still Rock and Roll to Me" singer Billy
16 Indians of the West
17 Immortal start for Caesar
18 Important ship of myth
19 I
22 It's in Lepus
23 Italian dish
24 Initials for a waitress
27 Ignorant reply
29 Individual who fishes
33 Interweave
38 "I Will __" (disco hit)
39 Intimate of Aeneas
40 Innermost orbital point
41 Influences in astrology
42 It precedes poetica
43 Irène's seasoning
44 Inventory, e.g.
48 Indonesian is similar to it
53 I
59 Infant's place
60 Innocent Hiss?
61 Item for heating liquids
62 Islets
63 Italian artist Andrea del __
64 Institutes legal action
65 It follows oom
66 In amongst
67 Intemperate fit

DOWN

1 Idolized drummer
2 "In Old Arizona," e.g.
3 Isaac the violinist
4 Idi __
5 Iberian "mouth"
6 Intense exam
7 Ideal, as greenhouse soil
8 Inspector
9 Idiot
10 Initiated
11 Isolated
13 In __ (actually)
15 Inamorata of Tarzan
20 Indispensable, in music
21 Introduction for an eye doctor
25 Instrument for lifting
26 "I think that I shall never see . . ." poem
27 Inferior cars
28 "I give!"
29 Itty-bitty meas.
30 Île de la Cité street
31 Ice hockey legend
32 Inscribed 56
34 Ill-looking
35 Inhabitant: Suffix
36 Income after taxes
37 Initial for Superman
44 Irving Berlin belonged to it
45 Israel-Turkey separator
46 Ian of Rhodesia
47 Inverse of "floods"
49 Iced drinks
50 Illuminated
51 It spans douze mois
52 It's uplifting
54 In the rear
55 Imperfection
56 Inhuman brute
57 Interconnection of nerves
58 Item in a laundry

by Bryant White   **Saturday, November 10, 1995**

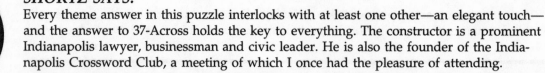

8

SHORTZ SAYS:
Every theme answer in this puzzle interlocks with at least one other—an elegant touch—and the answer to 37-Across holds the key to everything. The constructor is a prominent Indianapolis lawyer, businessman and civic leader. He is also the founder of the Indianapolis Crossword Club, a meeting of which I once had the pleasure of attending.

ACROSS

1 Geometry calculation
5 Mere tool
9 Cupid's master
14 Gun blast
15 Kyrgyzstan's __ Mountains
16 Athenian general
17 Yemeni city
18 Trapper's trophy
19 Gathered, as bees
20 37-Across from a 1953 western
23 Nonetheless
24 Not practice moderation
27 Carpenters, at times
31 Hopping __
32 Shopping aid
35 Twins. e.g.
36 Unattached
37 Theme of this puzzle
40 Doctrines
41 Philatelist's sheet
42 Radical Newton
43 Vane dir.
44 Dracula's home
46 More blessed
48 Sheriff's cry, in a western
53 37-Across from the cartoons
57 Moon over Uranus
59 Girlfriend abroad
60 Zola best seller
61 Trite
62 Swerve
63 Suffix with fabric or authentic
64 Upset
65 Loose items, sometimes
66 Stitches

DOWN

1 Rope plant
2 Home health hazard
3 The bad guys
4 Nixon Veep
5 Yellow fruit
6 Mr. Guinness
7 Alternative to hit
8 Louse eggs
9 Cold sorrel soups
10 Dress style
11 37-Across from a raven
12 Kicker's asset
13 Also
21 African tribe member
22 Actor __ Buchholz
25 A number 1
26 Works of Sappho
28 Belief of one billion
29 Climbing vine
30 "Barnaby Jones" star

32 Rodeo ring?
33 37-Across from a witch
34 Message in a bottle, maybe
36 Singer Christie
37 Christian symbol
38 Good-time Charlie
39 Place to see a catch
44 "Is that so!"
45 The unemployed
47 "Do __ a Waltz?"
49 Mrs. Chaplin and namesakes
50 Kind of glass
51 Words of understanding
52 Despots

54 Reliever's quest
55 "You said a mouthful"
56 Told a whopper
57 Legal org.
58 Fled or bled

by Michael S. Maurer   Thursday, December 7, 1995

SHORTZ SAYS:
Here is another puzzle with a mystery theme (see 36-Across), with six examples of it arranged in symmetrical positions around the grid. The constructor is an actuarial consultant in New York City. On a wall of his office at home hangs a giant crossword blanket of one of his puzzles—knitted by a fan.

ACROSS

1 Former Toyota model
6 Grenades, e.g.
10 This may be tiled
14 Church recesses
15 Roaster's place?
16 Humorist Bombeck
17 "Romeo and Juliet" event
18 Slight trace
20 Gaping, as the mouth
22 Dizziness
23 Bat wood
24 Indulge, in a way
26 Type of servitude
29 1 + 1= 3, for example
33 Noted name in puppetry
35 Buzzer
36 Theme of this puzzle
43 Birds __ feather
44 Woody vine
45 Trial conference
50 Whole lot of apples
54 Marilyn role
56 Transfer __
57 Actress De Mornay
59 Most lucid
62 Unfavorably known
64 Eastern princess
65 Swear
66 Spider nests
67 Trimming tools
68 Cross products
69 Narrow valley
70 Is not allowed to, for short

DOWN

1 Minor despot
2 Revolt
3 Analysis start
4 Breathing spell
5 Fictional wirehair

6 Source of TV revenue
7 Purple color
8 Chintzy ones
9 Fish-eating hawk
10 Enumerate
11 Not a copy: Abbr.
12 Melville classic
13 Cooler
19 "I'd consider __ honor"
21 Subject for Aristotle
25 __ Beach, Fla.
27 Brokaw's network
28 "Wonderful!"
30 Quick score in baseball
31 "I didn't know that!"

32 Approval
34 M - CCCL
36 Santa's laughs
37 "__ Loved You" ("Carousel" hit)
38 Bit
39 Bad check
40 Single-season home-run king
41 United
42 Churchill symbol
46 Jostles
47 Literally, farmer
48 Following a curve
49 Flinch
51 Violent agitation
52 Hidden
53 Fashion maven's quest

55 Honors word
57 Meander
58 __ collar
60 Composer Khachaturian
61 Zilch
62 Be off guard
63 Break a Commandment

by David J. Kahn   Wednesday, December 27, 1995

SHORTZ SAYS:
Cathy Millhauser is one of the funniest crossword constructors around, as well as one of the most elegant. Here she incorporates four familiar 15-letter phrases and gives them a punny twist.

ACROSS

1 Kickapoos, e.g.
6 "Tuna-Fishing" painter
10 Silent one
14 Emulated the Blob
15 "My People" author
16 Dash
17 Like well-behaved clerics?
20 Singular
21 Mirror backing
22 It can bring a tear to your eye
23 The Great Commoner
24 Spelling on TV
25 Like mosquitoes at a camp?
32 Pernod ingredient
33 Hoopster Archibald
34 "Who, Horatius?"
35 Baker or Battle, e.g.
36 Producers of bangs?
38 Swindle, slangily
39 Put away the dishes
40 Exec's dispatch
41 Pickle
42 Like tie-dyed clothes?
46 Hem
47 Fritzi, to Nancy
48 Sally
51 Mercyhurst College site
52 Indian sovereignty
55 Like Cinderella before the Prince?
58 Blue dye
59 Kind of thermometer
60 Ticket imperative
61 20's heavyweight Tunney
62 Street band
63 Goes the distance

DOWN

1 Fast food option
2 Crucifix
3 Shirt label
4 High-riser, e.g.
5 High-rise, e.g.
6 Danny of "Taxi"
7 Old actor Walter
8 __ Cruces
9 Mass sections
10 Deserved praise
11 O'Grady of "Eight is Enough"
12 Ham bits
13 Screen
18 Reply to the Little Red Hen
19 Seine feeder
23 City on the Arno
24 Pre-1917 ruler
25 One of Polly Adler's ilk
26 Grammy-winning Baker
27 Hepatologist's speciality
28 Washington's __ Station
29 Horse play?
30 "M*A*S*H" extra
31 Rake parts
36 Spinose mammal
37 Féminine friend
38 Junk
40 Ambulance driver
41 Dakar's land
43 Pot
44 Giving a darn
45 Trash
48 Decorative drapery
49 Caen's river
50 Harness part
51 Garden spot
52 __ horn (shofar)
53 Keep __ (persevere)
54 Jacuzzi set
56 60's singer Little __
57 Vitamin bottle abbr.

by Cathy Millhauser   Thursday, December 28, 1995

SHORTZ SAYS:
A mere glance at the clues below will reveal the unusual feature of this crossword. The answer at 40-Across spells it out. This puzzle is perfect proof that a crossword does not have to be hard to be ingenious or well-made.

ACROSS

1 __ Doc Duvalier
5 J. __ Hoover
10 __ au lait
14 __ Corporation (ammunition maker)
15 Jules __
16 __ friendly
17 "Of __ and Men"
18 "__ the news today . . ." (Beatles lyric)
19 "Take __ Train"
20 __ basket
22 "The __ Show on Earth"
24 "It's __ !" ("See you then!")
26 Camus's "The __ of Sisyphus"
27 __ so on
29 Nick at __
31 __ living
34 TV's "__ & Clark"
36 Hippocratic __
38 On the __
40 Title for this puzzle
43 "Van Gogh in __"
44 "Que __ . . ."
45 __ River, N.J.
46 __ the storm
48 Jay __
50 Jacqueline Kennedy, __ Bouvier
51 "__ Fiction"
53 British __
55 "The __ Heart"
59 Mount St. __
62 __ Canal
63 __ finish
65 Get __ the ground floor
66 "Rock of __"
67 __ nous
68 __ spumante
69 ". . . gathers no __"
70 __ the course (perseveres)
71 "Have a __"

DOWN

1 "__ and Circumstance"
2 Et __
3 __ Circus
4 Put __ to
5 __ notice
6 "__ Rosenkavalier"
7 Cyclist __ LeMond
8 __ and a leg
9 Take the __ (fly at night)
10 __ competition
11 Arthur __
12 Legal __
13 Quod __ demonstrandum
21 __ Fleming
23 "Not __" ("Thinking nothing of it")
25 __ Unis
27 __ Romeo
28 Bête __
30 __ Merman
32 __ panty hose
33 Billy Joel's "Don't __ Why"
35 "__ in Seattle"
37 "Ready or not, __ come!"
39 In __ (actually)
41 The word __
42 Rock's Siouxsie and the __
47 Go down in __
49 Grand __ Opry
52 Manufacturing __
54 __ Howe
55 __ player
56 "Cogito __ sum"
57 "True __"
58 __ Kett of the comics
60 __ bene
61 In a __ (agitated)
64 The old college __

by Martin Schneider

Monday, June 24, 1996

12

Perhaps my all-time favorite crossword in The Times. This originally appeared on the morning of Election Day in 1996, before the polls had opened across much of the country. Starting at about 9 A.M., and continuing all day, calls from outraged solvers poured into my office, because the callers assumed . . . well, you'll have to solve the puzzle to understand why. The puzzle was discussed on ABC's "World News Tonight" that night, and explained in The Times the next day.

ACROSS

1 "___ your name" (Mamas and Papas lyric)
6 Fell behind slightly
15 Euripides tragedy
16 Free
17 Forecast
19 Be bedridden
20 Journalist Stewart
21 Rosetta ___
22 1960's espionage series
24 ___ Perignon
25 Quilting party
26 "Drying out" program
28 Umpire's call
30 Tease
34 Tease
36 Standard
38 "The Tell-Tale Heart" writer
39 & 43 Lead story in tomorrow's newspaper (!)
45 Gold: Prefix
46 ___ Lee cakes
48 Bobble the ball
49 Spanish aunts
51 Obi
53 Bravery
57 Small island
59 Daddies
61 Theda of 1917's "Cleopatra"
62 Employee motivator
65 Otherworldly
67 Treasure hunter's aid
68 Title for 39-Across next year
71 Exclusion from social events
72 Fab Four name
73 They may get tied up in knots
74 Begin, as a maze

DOWN

1 Disable
2 Cherry-colored
3 Newspaperman Ochs
4 Easel part
5 Actress Turner
6 Ropes, as dogies
7 Place to put your feet up
8 Underskirt
9 First of three-in-a-row
10 Lower in public estimation
11 Onetime bowling alley employee
12 Threesome
13 English prince's school
14 60's TV talk-show host Joe
18 Superannuated
23 Sewing shop purchase
25 TV's Uncle Miltie
27 Short writings
29 Opponent
31 Likely
32 Actress Caldwell
33 End of the English alphabet
35 Trumpet
37 Ex-host Griffin
39 Black Halloween animal
40 French 101 word
41 Provider of support, for short
42 Much-debated political inits.
44 Sourpuss
47 Malign
50 "La Nausee" novelist
52 Sheik's cliques
54 Bemoan
55 Popsicle color
56 Bird of prey
58 10 on a scale of 1 to 10
60 Family girl
62 Famous ___
63 Something to make on one's birthday
64 Regarding
65 Quite a story
66 Dublin's land
69 ___ Victor
70 Hullabaloo

by Jeremiah Farrell   Tuesday, November 5, 1996

SHORTZ SAYS:

Five theme answers, arranged in order from top to bottom (and covering all the possibilities of the theme), make this puzzle remarkable. The constructor, a high school math teacher in Brooklyn, N.Y., has six crosswords in the book—more than any other person.

13

ACROSS

1 Certain drapes
6 Atlantic food fish
10 Gator's kin
14 Cop __ (confess for a lighter sentence)
15 White-tailed flier
16 Deli offering
17 Colt 45, e.g.
19 List member
20 "That's a lie!"
21 Household
23 70's–80's robotic rock group
25 The United States, metaphorically
27 Uris hero
28 Dance, in Dijon
29 Member of the 500 HR club
30 Rock impresario Brian
31 Surgical fabric
33 Ant, in dialect
35 "Texaco Star Theater" host
39 Cut down
40 Brilliance
43 High dudgeon
46 Mai __
47 Go on to say
49 "Bravo!"
50 It once settled near Pompeii
53 Part of a whole
54 Kangaroo moves
55 Hayfield activity
57 Prefix with China
58 Kind of cereal
62 Shade of red
63 Conception
64 Bizarre
65 Bronte heroine
66 Pre-1821 Missouri, e.g.: Abbr.
67 He had Scarlett fever

DOWN

1 Uncle of note
2 New Deal prog.
3 Stream deposit
4 "I can't __" (Stones refrain)
5 Morton product
6 "Rocky II," e.g.
7 Diabolical
8 Due halved
9 Words of assistance
10 "I __" (ancient Chinese text)
11 Record again
12 Where to find Eugene
13 Awaken
18 Early Shirley role
22 Signed up for
23 U.N.'s Hammarskjold
24 Former polit. cause
26 __ of the Unknowns
28 Like some greeting cards
32 Nine-digit number, maybe
33 Ultimate point
34 R.N.'s offering
36 Send
37 Trompe l'__
38 Stretch
41 He KO'd Quarry, 10/26/70
42 Asian holiday
43 Tipple
44 "Didja ever wonder . . . ?" humorist
45 Successful escapee
47 Incarnation
48 Spanish Surrealist
51 Certain investment, informally
52 More competent
53 Jesse who lost to Ronald Reagan in 1970
56 Composer Stravinsky
59 Ending with quiet
60 N.Y.C. subway
61 Modern information source, with "the"

by Alan Arbesfeld

Tuesday, March 11, 1997

SHORTZ SAYS:

(14) David Kahn never makes an ordinary puzzle, but this one is truly exceptional. Every theme answer (four horizontal and two vertical) interlocks with at least one other, and the answer at 7-Down gives a playful explanation of what these six have in common.

ACROSS

1 Construction lifts
7 "If __ a nickel . . ."
11 Pointed criticism
14 You can say that again!
15 Section flanked by aisles
16 Hubbub
17 Appoint
18 Spring zoo attraction
20 Tick off
21 Dearie
22 Ambles (along)
23 Magellan, e.g.
27 Crescent-shaped figure
28 Olive __
29 Beach time in Buenos Aires
32 Retired
33 Struggle
34 O'Brien of "The Barefoot Contessa"
36 TV news time
37 Namesakes of a literary fox
39 Suffix with saw
40 Plain homes
42 Eight pts.
43 Not occurring naturally
44 __ voce
45 Adaptable truck, for short
46 Stonewort, e.g.
47 Confederate soldier, at times?
50 Pundit
53 Where to hear "All Things Considered"
54 Number of articles in the Constitution
55 New York City opera benefactor?
57 Melon originally from Turkey
60 Tide rival

61 Noted first name in jazz
62 Like Alban Berg's music
63 Get spliced
64 __-poly
65 Metric units

DOWN

1 Med. care provider
2 Sweep
3 World's fair pavilion
4 Famished
5 Tot's transport
6 Start of many Western place names
7 Theme of this puzzle
8 1492 Columbus discovery
9 Dow Jones fig.
10 Pool areas
11 Item in a trunk
12 Together, musically
13 Feints in boxing
19 "Air Music" composer
21 Contribute, as to an account
23 Criticize in no uncertain terms
24 Red corundums
25 Continues
26 Razzed
30 Louis XIV, to himself?
31 Wound up
35 Cheerless
37 Attorney's request
38 Critic
41 Old words from which modern words are derived
43 Half of the Odd Couple
48 Sound of passage
49 Not perfectly round
50 Fish-eating duck
51 Ginger Rogers tune "__ in the Money"
52 Not much
56 Day-__
57 Be-bopper
58 "Phooey!"
59 Capp and Capone

by David J. Kahn

Thursday, May 8, 1997

SHORTZ SAYS:

Did I get mail after publishing this puzzle! Many solvers didn't understand the theme even after seeing the answer . . . although most seemed to appreciate it when it was explained. (See the note in the back of the book in case you're stymied, too.) This was the only crossword that Isabel Walcott ever had published in The Times. In fact, if I remember correctly, it's the only one she ever submitted.

ACROSS

1 Like The Citadel, now
5 The Constitution, e.g.
9 Wing it
14 Fit
15 Place for a pig
16 Metier
17 With 35-Down, a birth announcement
18 Place to hold a banquet roast?
19 Like some diseases
20 Heavy-duty kitchen implement
22 Rebound
23 60's sitcom that had a whistled intro, with "The"
28 Prepare to share
32 Circumference
33 Sheik's peer
34 March V.I.P.
35 N₂O, e.g.
38 What a "choosy mother" might pack for lunch
42 Ninny
43 CompuServe service
44 Wit Bombeck
45 Winter Palace residents
46 Put on ice
48 Unsavory MTV cartoon duo
52 Chevy rival
53 Familiar five-word phrase that means "Excuses are unacceptable!"
58 Staffers
60 Abominable Snowman
62 Turnoff
63 Reinstates
64 Dark __
65 Southwestern sight
66 Elliptical
67 Crawl
68 Black

DOWN

1 Smart
2 Swear word
3 Otherwise
4 Sugar substitute?
5 Mooch
6 Remain in an uncertain state
7 "Crusade in Europe" author, familiarly
8 Place for a pig
9 Recreational four-wheeler, for short
10 Least sweet
11 Durable wood
12 Where Shoshone Falls falls
13 Not on deck
21 "The Spanish Tragedy" dramatist
24 Rather stout
25 Press on
26 Alpine elevator
27 Billboard listings
28 __ vu
29 Troublemakers
30 Struggles
31 Stash for cash, briefly
34 Maze word
35 See 17-Across
36 Tiptop
37 Roe source
39 40's theater director James
40 Thurman et al.
41 Cause of a fly's demise
45 Idiot boxes
46 The way and the path
47 They might be zapped
48 Crow
49 Type of type
50 Milk snake
51 Keypad key
54 This might be in for the long haul
55 Farm team
56 Put on the line
57 Corset part
59 Mariner's dir.
60 Deviation at sea
61 Psychology I

by Isabel Walcott

Saturday, May 10, 1997

16

ACROSS

1 "Buffalo ___" (1844 song)
5 Speleologist
10 Guinea pigs, maybe
14 Tissue additive
15 Departure
16 Departure
17 Puccini soprano
18 Father of William the Conqueror
19 Anna Leonowens, e.g., in "The King and I"
20 They make wakeup calls
22 "Memphis ___" (1990 war film)
23 Drench, in a way
24 Hurt
26 Stocks and such
29 Tries
30 Whiskered animal
31 Stuck, after "in"
32 "The lie that enables us to realize the truth": Picasso
35 Shakespeare classic
39 Hurricane heading: Abbr.
40 Petrol unit
41 Kennedy's Secretary of State
42 Jibe
43 Calm
45 Severe critic
48 Star witnesses?
49 Actress Barkin
50 Parting word
54 Whim
55 Cast
57 Casa material
58 Mount whose name means "I burn"
59 Jackson and Jefferson, e.g.
60 "Mona ___"
61 Spots

62 ___ Rose
63 Pipe piece

DOWN

1 Gainesville athlete
2 "Not to mention . . ."
3 Wacky
4 Scallop, for one
5 Special touch
6 Cherish
7 They may be picked up
8 Poetic adverb
9 Sticking point
10 Hollywood producer Jon
11 Rejoice
12 King, for instance
13 Kept on the hard drive
21 Kindergartener
22 Genesis city
24 Wrap
25 Where Timbuktu is
26 Former Davis Cup captain
27 Writer O'Faolain
28 The very ___
29 Beach
31 It has many narrow rays
32 A pastel
33 Deteriorate
34 Kindergartener
36 Former Laker great Baylor
37 Cross-ply, e.g.
38 You can count on them
42 Circus sites
43 States as fact
44 I
45 Indicates
46 Blue bloods
47 Replicate
48 Best Picture of 1955
50 Chimney-top nester
51 Mine entrance
52 Rocketed
53 Nautical direction
55 Nautical direction
56 Bird sound

by Randall J. Hartman

Thursday, July 24, 1997

SHORTZ SAYS:
The most successful punny puzzles are the ones that make you laugh, and this one's a good example. It features six theme answers with a very specific phonetic twist.

ACROSS

1 Grist for processors
5 Quizzes
9 Hurt
14 "L'__ c'est moi": Louis XIV
15 Train transportation
16 Word in a Yale song
17 Religious monster?
19 Sound louder than kerplop
20 Swimming pool problem
21 Athos, Porthos and Aramis, e.g.
23 1944 Pulitzer journalist
24 It's rolled out at parties
26 Wooden shoe
28 1940's Big-Band leader
30 Solidarnosc leader
33 Chattering birds
36 Not stiff
38 Frothy
39 Serpent's mark?
40 Popular men's magazine
42 Parisian way
43 "Mefistofele" composer
45 Biology subj.
46 Gets choked up
47 Charles's "Gaslight" co-star, 1944
49 "__ to bed"
51 Solicit cash from
53 Formation of bone
57 Spoils
59 Cream of the crop
61 Junta's act
62 Tigger's adopted mom
64 Macho dance?
66 Signed
67 Sound
68 December air
69 Compote fruit
70 Q-Tip
71 In __ (existing)

DOWN

1 Make lean?
2 "I could __ unfold . . .": "Hamlet"
3 Northern evergreen forests
4 Jumps on
5 S.A. republic
6 Patron of bread?
7 Narc's catch, maybe
8 Putdowns
9 Tummy muscles
10 "Apocalypse Now" director
11 Jerusalem?
12 One way to get to Jerusalem
13 Anniversary, e.g.
18 Take, as oral arguments
22 Cut
25 Wear the crown
27 Barbara, to friends
29 Popular appliance maker
31 Overproud
32 Words said in passing?
33 Skater Thomas
34 Shakespeare, the Bard of __
35 Measure a pop singer?
37 Musical fish?
40 "Go ahead!"
41 Some old Fords
44 Set off
46 "Nice going!"
48 Name
50 Kind of aerobics
52 Pains in the neck
54 Farm towers
55 F.D.R.'s Interior Secretary
56 Several-days-old
57 Pass over
58 Diminish
60 Pack away
63 TV breaks
65 Miss out?

by Karen Hodge

Wednesday, September 17, 1997

SHORTZ SAYS:
This is the first and (so far) only crossword in The Times by this puzzle whiz in his 20's, who won a prize as a solver at a recent American Crossword Puzzle Tournament. His puzzle utilizes a common theme element in four different ways as it tests your mind's ability to be flexible.

ACROSS

1 Radio station supply
6 Dismay
10 Louis who was guillotined
13 Flu ward sound
14 "You said it!"
15 Regular Cosmo feature
16 Betraying, briefly
18 Lhasa __ (dog)
19 Colony member
20 Strove (for)
21 Told (on)
23 Advance
24 Antigun lobbyist Brady
25 Congresswoman Waters
28 Respectful
31 Commencement
32 Wizards
33 Prevent
34 Four on a four, e.g.
35 Tint
36 Coffee
37 Nationality suffix
38 Flapjack places, for short
39 Punished, perhaps
40 Like some pizzas
42 Punish, perhaps
43 Speak monotonously
44 Soothing instrument
45 Knee/ankle connector
47 Glow
48 "Look here!"
51 Eager
52 It indicates what's happening, briefly
55 Womanizer
56 Raison d'__
57 Bud Grace comic strip
58 Unified
59 Antique store tag
60 Kind of statement

DOWN

1 Arp art
2 What a model might become
3 Barricade, with "in"
4 Inner ear
5 In the black, like a dry cleaner?
6 Sent, in a way
7 Within
8 Form of Buddhism
9 Currier or Ives
10 Start playing, briefly
11 Tight gripper
12 __ Lacoste
15 Mideast nation
17 "__ kleine Nachtmusik"
22 God shown with a burning torch
23 "Fairy tales"
24 Utah lilies
25 Two-wheeler
26 Liqueur flavor
27 Two-wheeler, briefly
28 "Lord of the Flies" leader
29 Object of contemplation?
30 Business
32 Bullwinkle, for one
35 Waters off Hong Kong
36 Green shade
38 Pop star, say
39 Wine orders
41 Bluenose
42 Lighting specialist, informally?
44 Crescents
45 Betting game
46 Tolstoy hero
47 Prefix with culture
48 "Yikes!"
49 Son, usually
50 Farm team
53 "__ a Joke, Son" (1947 flick)
54 Big inits. in credit reporting

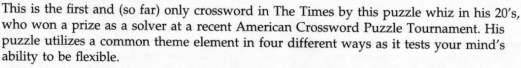

by Kiran S. Kedlaya   **Thursday, November 27, 1997**

SHORTZ SAYS:
According to my rules, a crossword does not need a theme if it contains 72 or fewer entries. This brilliant construction by a young mathematician contains just 68 entries, yet has six theme answers.

ACROSS

1 Kind of wrench
7 Venomous, as a snake
13 Do well
14 Not real
16 Reducer
17 Eavesdropped
19 With 49-Across, underlying theme of 24-Down
21 Prefix with stasis
22 "__ only"
23 Appropriate, in a way
25 School subj.
26 Hall of fame
28 Brine-cured cheeses
30 The skeptic
32 Hairy-chested
33 With the worst consequences
35 Convictions
36 __ Foods, Inc.
37 Frequent 24-Down subject
38 Picture
39 Public relations interpretations
40 Undermine
41 Vituperates
43 Gift __
47 Site of temptation
49 See 19-Across
52 Nice work if you can get it
54 James Russell Lowell, for one
55 Freshens, in a way
56 Bow out
57 Illegal race track workers
58 Secret fraternity

DOWN

1 Put on
2 "Goody!"
3 Desire
4 Wind-up toys?
5 Incessantly
6 Arctic __
7 Very much
8 Climb
9 Wallop
10 Some investors' income: Abbr.
11 Pipe part
12 Truthful qualities
15 Actress Laurie of "Roseanne"
18 Parts of meeting rooms
20 Hairy-chested
24 Theme of this puzzle, with "The"
26 The believer
27 Spanish stew
29 Object of March celebrations
30 Made more precipitous
31 "Double Indemnity" novelist
32 Phlebotomy target
33 Defensive ditches
34 Land of peace and simplicity
35 Heaven
37 Relevance
39 Bothersome bedmate
42 Critical
43 Fieri facias and others
44 Statistical bit
45 It's put away for winter
46 Mourning sites
48 Student of Seneca
50 Give a wave?
51 Essay's basis
53 Kind of gun

by Ed Pegg Jr.

Friday, November 28, 1997

SHORTZ SAYS:
In fall 1997 a young Manhattan lawyer, Bill Gottlieb, called me at The Times, asking if I would be willing to run a crossword containing a marriage proposal to his crossword-loving girlfriend, Emily Mindel. The puzzle below, which I specially commissioned from Bob Klahn, was the result. Over breakfast with Bill on the day this was first published, Emily solved the puzzle and said "57-Down!" The couple appeared on numerous television shows about their unusual engagement. I attended their wedding, and Bob and I have heard from Bill and Emily on every anniversary since the puzzle appeared.

ACROSS

1 "High Hopes" lyricist
5 __ Romeo
9 Pull oneself up to the bar
13 Mélange
14 Microsoft chief, to some
16 "Darling, Je Vous __ Beaucoup"
17 Answers, for short
18 Poet Dickinson
19 Dirty Harry's employer: Abbr.
20 1729 Jonathan Swift pamphlet, with "A"
23 Old enough to know better?
24 Pork place?
25 Frasier's brother
27 Highly rated
29 Begin again
30 Cosby series
33 Without whiskers
37 Key or Kennedy
38 1965 Gary Lewis and the Playboys hit
41 "2001" mainframe
42 Fluster
43 Chip for a pot
44 Crater Lake locale
46 Obi-__ Kenobi
48 Ennui, to Enrique
49 Stat. for Barry Bonds
52 Fall guy
56 1992 Paula Abdul hit, with Stevie Wonder on harmonica
59 Listen and obey
60 Take the honey and run
61 Driver's selection
62 Suffix with bachelor
63 Comparatively cagey
64 Collate
65 Like show horses
66 Cold capital
67 Artist Paul

DOWN

1 Popular women's mag
2 Reserved
3 Broom __ (comics witch)
4 Posies
5 Help at a heist
6 Proceeds falteringly
7 Play at love
8 Brass or bronze
9 Black currant liqueur
10 Pompous
11 Carry out
12 Stephen Foster's "Old Uncle __"
15 Bilk, say
21 Melville setting
22 Erect
26 Bulrush, e.g.
28 Like some flu
29 Ask for more Time?
30 "Some Like __"
31 Offer some to
32 Entered en masse
34 This may be over your head
35 Tbsp. or tsp.
36 Radio setting: Abbr.
39 Covet, with "over"
40 Threw caution to the wind
45 Like some lilies
47 Shower time: Abbr.
49 Rich kid in "Nancy"
50 Encourages, with "up"
51 Push forward
53 Its capital is Innsbruck
54 Chocolate marshmallow snack
55 "Fiddler on the Roof" matchmaker
57 Hoped-for response to 56-Across
58 Dynamic start
59 Enero, por ejemplo

by Bob Klahn   **Wednesday, January 7, 1998**

SHORTZ SAYS:

This beautifully crafted puzzle uses its theme element nine times in a total of 18 answers. What makes the grid particularly elegant is that these theme elements appear in perfectly symmetric positions.

ACROSS

1. Under __ (concealed)
6. Woman's shoe
10. "Cease and desist!"
14. Irene, Dike and Eunomia
15. Positive
16. Stigma
17. Spooky board
18. Kind of list
19. __ Beauty (apple variety)
20. "Finally!"
22. Food
24. Honest one
25. __ & Chandon (champagne)
27. Diamond middleman?
29. Herb sometimes called Chinese parsley
33. For example
34. Computer type
35. Writer Jaffe
37. Fixed tire
41. __ foo yung
42. Coroner's concern
44. "Eureka!"
45. Frothy
48. Way of speaking
49. Formal hat, informally
50. Lawyer's hurdle
52. Frightening
54. First-rate
58. Korean statesman
59. __ Tomé and Principe
60. College sports org.
62. Disgust
66. Polo competitor
68. Summit
70. Bellyache
71. Nimble
72. Football's Armstrong
73. Later
74. Hinders legally
75. Corset prop
76. Cooped up at Old MacDonald's

DOWN

1. "Hold it!"
2. Beat badly
3. Seed covering
4. Bit of bedwear
5. Rainy or silly follower
6. Camera setting
7. Pear-shaped instrument
8. Spheres
9. Tithe amounts
10. Abbr. on old Asian maps
11. Paint job finale
12. Pentameter parts
13. Questionable cradle location
21. Aquarium fish
23. Glide aloft
26. "Speckled" fish
28. Bread for a Reuben
29. G __
30. Betrayer of the Moor
31. Women's Tour sponsor: Abbr.
32. Fully informed about
36. Ed of "Lou Grant"
38. Mob boss
39. Doubt-conveying interjection
40. Peel
43. Refrain in many early Beatles songs
46. Entrepreneur's deg.
47. Gape
49. Hush-hush
51. Right-hand pages
53. Rules
54. Up on deck
55. Stuns
56. Locale for Santa's team
57. Singer Bonnie
61. Samoan capital
63. Fuzzy fruit
64. Sporting rapier
65. Bookworm
67. Toper's woe
69. Stowe girl

by Susan Smith

Wednesday, March 18, 1998

(22)

ACROSS

1 Kind of shower
7 Bedroom furniture
14 Treat with gas
15 "Gunsmoke" deputy
16 Mythical warrior
17 Consolidated clockmaker?
19 Give off
21 Teachers' org.
22 Cleopatra biter
23 Oldenburg "oh!"
26 Private reply, maybe
28 Oktoberfest supply
29 Valerie Harper TV role
32 Start of many ship names
33 "Peter Pan" heroine
34 Consolidated composer?
37 Decree
38 Popular radio format
42 Consolidated singer?
46 Wistful exclamation
49 Stir
50 Accepted rule
51 Actor's goal
52 Office folk
54 Literary monogram
55 Yalie
56 Ally of the Fox tribe
57 Kismet
60 Consolidated puzzle author?
63 Mountainous
67 Distinguished
68 Headline-making weather phenomenon
69 Deviation
70 Places to sit, paradoxically

DOWN

1 Cry to Bo-peep
2 "Losing My Religion" rock group
3 Brother of 34-Across
4 Stun
5 Focus for Fermi
6 Red Square figure
7 Heat beaters: Abbr.
8 Like Cologne and environs
9 Taxi feature
10 Workplace regulator, for short
11 "What was __ think?"
12 Stay
13 Eliminated, in a way
18 Like a little old lady in tennis shoes?
20 Hit the road
23 Ship on which Heracles sailed
24 "Moonstruck" star
25 Cascades mount
27 Induction grp.
28 Former aerospace giant
30 Adorned, in a way
31 Light-footed
33 Mrs. Flintstone
35 Alfonso XIII's queen
36 Court
39 Brief O.K.: Abbr.
40 They can be bruised
41 Between 0% and 100%
43 Jeer
44 Cretan peak
45 Remove
46 Couturier Cassini
47 Mother of Constantine the Great
48 Get closer to, in a race
52 Brazilian dance
53 Passengers
56 Dog-paddled, e.g.
58 Conclusion of some games
59 Poet __ St. Vincent Millay
61 Ike's W.W. II command
62 Marshal under Napoleon
64 Conclusion of some games
65 Conclusion
66 Bits of advice

by Gene Newman

Wednesday, March 25, 1998

SHORTZ SAYS:
A crossword with only 66 answers—and a theme besides—is pretty extraordinary by any standard. The puzzle's lively nontheme answers (like 54-Across, 2-Down and 32-Down) make it even nicer.

23

ACROSS

1 Loopy
7 Some roads
15 Montana strip
16 #13
17 More than just a fight
19 Abridged
20 Bill in Washington?
21 Old English length
22 Word with jacket or coal
23 Unabridged
24 Dismounted
25 Seafood entree
28 Big name in pet foods
29 Moreover
30 Small logging operator
31 1907–8 Series winner
34 Classified abbr.
36 Presumptive explorer?
39 Supermarket head
43 "The Mocker Mocked" artist, 1930
44 Strip
45 Many Trekkie costumes
46 Suffix with form
47 Saw
48 "Is that __?"
49 What FEMA provides
54 Lawn barrow feature
55 Certain gardener
56 Swords and such
57 Fleet

DOWN

1 Marked time
2 Place for a markdown
3 "Strange as it may seem . . ."
4 Confab
5 A abroad
6 Think worthy of doing
7 Resin used in varnishes
8 Remodels, e.g.
9 Vituperate
10 __ Darya (Asian river)
11 Like
12 "Measure for Measure" villain
13 Chris of the N.B.A.
14 Troutlike fish
18 Part of a Dr. Seuss title
22 The usual
23 Put away, in a way
24 Quantum

26 Frolicking, after "on"
27 Spot
32 Prude
33 Like a pie chart
35 Cooler
36 Punches
37 Hymns of thanksgiving
38 "You betcha!"
39 Football's Fighting __
40 Left off
41 Ransom
42 Knots
43 Praise
48 Polygonal recess
50 Amaze
51 __ Na Na

52 Kind of culture
53 Adjudge

by David J. Kahn

Saturday, March 28, 1998

24

SHORTZ SAYS:
This puzzle and the one for the following day (see next page) go together as a pair. You should solve this one first.

ACROSS

1 Check
5 Fill to excess
9 Country bumpkin
13 Pretentious
14 Deposed leader's fate, maybe
16 Chester Arthur's middle name
17 ◇
20 Airport info, informally
21 On the safe side, at sea
22 Math groups
23 Here, to Henri
24 Calcutta clothing
25 □
33 Klingon or Vulcan
34 Women's group?
35 Coach Parseghian
36 Buster Brown's dog
37 Central points
38 First governor of Alaska
39 Loser to R.M.N. in '68
40 Numbers game
41 Sharp
42 ○
45 One who's on your side
46 London lav
47 Bother
50 In a frenzy
52 Take a part
55 △
58 Lago contents
59 Seasonal visitor
60 Efficient
61 Actress Schneider
62 Hoot
63 Not a hit or an out

DOWN

1 "Streamers" playwright David
2 Part of Q.E.D.
3 Frank Capra's "__ Wonderful Life"
4 Bill __, the Science Guy
5 Protect, as freshness
6 Bridge toll unit
7 Floor unit
8 Actor Wallach
9 Kind of bread
10 1997 Peter Fonda title role
11 Latvian, e.g.
12 Volumes A and Z in an encyclopedia
15 Boxes
18 Part of a hearty breakfast
19 Discussion medium
23 "Mm-hmm!"
24 Somewhat
25 Prefix with logical
26 Peace Nobelist Root
27 "Oh, sure"
28 Yankee Hall-of-Famer Ford
29 Must
30 International court site, with "The"
31 Plenty sore
32 Jury
37 Atheistic
38 Return to the Alps?
40 French textile city
41 Came to
43 Square dance move
44 Baseball's Roberto
47 Frost
48 Jason's ship
49 Refuse
50 "Rule, Britannia" composer
51 "G'day" recipient
52 Palindromic pop group
53 It makes a bit of a stir
54 Hard journey
56 __ Mahal
57 Stomach

by Alan Arbesfeld

Tuesday, March 31, 1998

Nearly every April 1 the Times crossword has some sort of April Fool's joke, and this one was a classic. On March 31 and April 1, 1998, the puzzles were by the same constructor, had the same pattern of black-and-white squares, had the same four visual theme clues and shared their first three Across clues. In other words, at first glance they looked identical. Many solvers assumed that The Times had made an error and accidentally reprinted the March 31 puzzle on April 1. But in fact the two puzzles are completely different. Ha, ha. April fools!

ACROSS

1 Check
5 Fill to excess
9 Country bumpkin
13 New Jersey city
14 All-night teen parties
16 Send off
17 ◇
20 Lilliputian
21 Ready to serve
22 They're trouble for roses
23 Bass, for one
24 __ Fox
25 □
33 Honeydew, e.g.
34 Spa
35 Excessively
36 Parched
37 Bug
38 One of Columbus's ships
39 Words at the altar
40 Senator John
41 Like a shoe
42 ○
45 Peaches
46 Idiom: Abbr.
47 Sound choice
50 Look
52 1936 candidate Landon
55 △
58 Sounds from Hawaii
59 Legend in automotives
60 Top spot
61 Meal eaten in a hall
62 They get in the way of sound thinking
63 More than lean

DOWN

1 Great deal
2 Character
3 Lip
4 "Mamma __!"
5 Dishes with syrup
6 Hardly believable
7 Pizza place
8 Money for a Toyota, say
9 One of the Beverly Hillbillies
10 Mine, in Marseille
11 Species
12 Alpine off-seasons
15 Stiff
18 __ Heights
19 Viewfinders?
23 Give __ to (approve)
24 Relay sticks
25 Screen letters
26 "Rigoletto" composer
27 "The Hollow Men" poet
28 Doubleday and others
29 Fran Drescher TV role
30 Beneficial
31 Fair-sized musical group
32 Parasite
37 Colorado city on the Rio Grande
38 Film genre
40 Actress Garson
41 Jerk
43 Way out
44 Works by 26-Down
47 Pigsty
48 Puff
49 Party times
50 Complacent
51 River in Spain
52 Purina competitor
53 Mortgage
54 Good-lookin'
56 Secure, as a victory
57 Prattle

by Alan Arbesfeld

Wednesday, April 1, 1998

SHORTZ SAYS:
At the time of publication, this puzzle tied a record for the lowest number of black squares ever used in a standard 15×15-square American crossword. To achieve this feat, Manny Nosowsky used two sets of triply-stacked answers at the top and bottom of the grid, all of them lively words and phrases. Altogether he spent almost 100 hours constructing the grid.

ACROSS

1 Some noncoms
16 Risking danger
17 So as to annoy
18 Cheerful
19 Leave a mess
20 Some docs
21 Biscuit ingredient
22 Kind of col. or cmdr.
23 Start of a carol's refrain
24 British verb ending
25 Bruce of old movies
26 Basque topper
27 They're spotted in Africa
29 Salt of element #5
30 Forward
31 Resting place
32 Neglectful
35 Big Apple V.I.P.
39 Pitch
40 Jai alai basket
41 Skedaddle
42 Odd and even, at times
43 Severe blows
44 Smoother
45 Milk source
46 Truman's birthplace
47 "The __ Kid"
48 Some Slim Fast offerings
51 Distractive annoyance
52 Impatience

DOWN

1 Emitting noxious fumes
2 Torture
3 The "Incredible Hulk" creator
4 Reflect
5 Part of a choosing-up routine
6 Literary inits.
7 Be patient
8 "Specials," often
9 Drag off again
10 "Whither thou __ . . ."
11 What I must follow, in a children's song
12 It borders the Atl.
13 Western New York county
14 One with instant siblings
15 Having feeling
22 Tellers of tales
23 Iron-containing: Prefix
25 Protested event
26 When repeated, a college cheer
28 "How the West Was Won" and others
29 Matches
31 The 51st Psalm
32 Diane's successor on "Cheers"
33 Utopian novel of 1872
34 Dispense, as small shares
35 Form of some dynamite
36 __ king crab
37 Emerging
38 Duties
40 Chevrolet introduced in 1966
43 Second-century anatomist
44 Cowboy's rope
46 French novelist Pierre
47 China problem
49 Brain and spinal cord: Abbr.
50 Grads-to-be

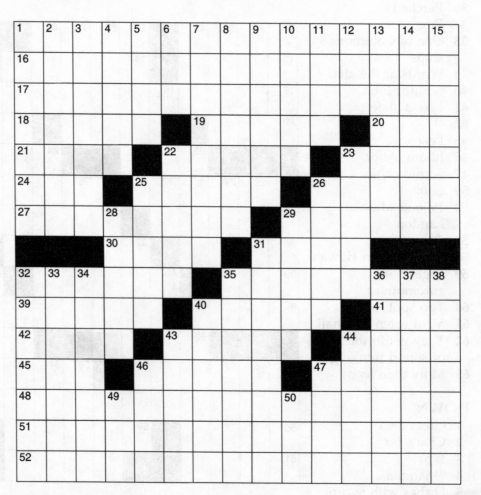

by Manny Nosowsky

Friday, July 24, 1998

SHORTZ SAYS:

The diabolical Henry Hook has legions of fans in the puzzle world. His crosswords appear every other week in the Sunday Boston Globe. He is also the author of numerous puzzle books. Fortunately for you, this is a milder example of his work ("HH lite," as it were), featuring an amusing theme pulled from everyday life.

ACROSS

1 Redcap's burden
5 No Westminster contender
9 Kind of tide
13 Condominium, e.g.
14 "__, of golden daffodils": Wordsworth
16 Plead for
17 Prefix with marketing
18 Author Lofts
19 Exactly
20 Ad line #1
23 ". . . fish __ fowl"
24 Caviar, once
25 Ad line #2
34 Boston Tea Party V.I.P.
35 Parts of cloverleafs
36 Margery of nursery rhymedom
37 Jam ingredient?
38 Fussbudget
39 VIII septupled
40 __ roll
41 One who makes dreams come true
42 Stringent
44 Ad line #3
47 Every last iota
48 Canal site
49 Ad line #4
57 Boggy area, for short
58 Remark heard at quitting time?
59 Warrior of legend
61 Loosen
62 Served as gondolier
63 Limp watch painter
64 Org.
65 Battle the clock
66 Portraitist's medium

DOWN

1 Word preceding 20-Across
2 From square one
3 Colorado feeder
4 Ms. founder
5 You can say that again!
6 "Oops!"
7 Ignored the speed limit
8 Autocrat
9 Eggnog enhancement
10 Slangy suffix
11 1934 Pulitzer winner Herbert
12 St. __ (vacation spot)
15 It could be a group effort
21 Turn's partner
22 Boozers
25 Georgia city not in its namesake county
26 Town in a 1944 novel
27 Fort Knox unit
28 The old nine-to-five
29 Spoke more than once?
30 Saxony seaport
31 Goldbrick
32 Star QB of Super Bowl XXXI
33 Doublemint figures
38 Bankrupt
41 "A good walk spoiled," said Twain
42 P.D.Q., on "ER"
43 Transport to Oz
45 Broadway setting since 4/11/91
46 Become an exmember
49 Blue hue
50 "The Sound of Music" extras
51 Root beer brand
52 __ about (roughly)
53 Where Bill Walton played
54 One of the Baldwins
55 Santa Barbara suburb
56 The Great __
60 Omicrons' predecessors

by Henry Hook   **Thursday, August 27, 1998**

28

ACROSS

1 95501
9 Smiling, for now
15 Topical
16 Avoidance
17 97401
18 16501
19 Tongue's locale
20 Actress Thompson
22 Dict. listing
23 Telephoned
27 Drop shot
29 Rosemary portrayer
32 54703
37 Odd
39 R. J. Reynolds brand
40 River of Belgium
41 Theme of this puzzle?
44 Lover of fur?
45 Headed off on
47 Very hot
49 80110
52 Give the once-over
53 Majestic swimmer
54 Case for small scissors
56 Stomach
59 Group
61 __ Nostra
65 73701
67 08818
71 Aplenty
72 Madness
73 Go to
74 79910

DOWN

1 Summers abroad
2 "Nope"
3 __ Park, Queens
4 Arabian title
5 Kal __ Foods, Inc.
6 Put away
7 A.F.L.'s partner
8 Field size, maybe
9 Lack of vitality
10 Actor Rick
11 Prefix with directional
12 Pleads
13 Perceive
14 __ of admissions
21 Year in the reign of Edward VI
24 Atmosphere: Prefix
25 Reputation
26 Southernmost of the Marianas
28 Big name in cheese
29 Wishy-washy reply
30 "The Wild Duck" playwright
31 Lay __ (flop)
33 Mild cigar
34 "Dallas" Miss
35 Pipsqueak
36 Portrait
38 Certain exams
42 French antiseptic
43 Milk: Prefix
46 Recent arrival
48 Trifle
50 Threw four balls at
51 Plastic __ Band
55 They stand for something
56 Prefix with store
57 Sci. course
58 Weaken
60 Transfer
62 Aware of
63 Huffy state
64 Sophocles tragedy
66 Universal John
68 "Runaway" singer __ Shannon
69 Mischievous one
70 Pirate's home, with "the"

by Alan Arbesfeld

Thursday, October 8, 1998

SHORTZ SAYS:
This visually striking grid contains only 19 Across answers (no standard American-style crossword has ever had fewer), yet is filled with fresh, colorful vocabulary. By the way, a crossword pattern like this, containing many straight edges, is far more difficult to construct than one with the more traditional stairstep pattern of black squares.

ACROSS

1 It'll give you an even split
9 Hello and goodbye
15 "Heat" star, 1995
16 European capital
17 Was taught how to do something
19 Result of a buyout, perhaps
20 Some hummingbirds
21 Humble beginning
28 Vice President under Grover Cleveland
36 Extended patience, perhaps
37 Get all gussied up
38 Lesser Spanish noblemen
39 Revolver feature, perhaps
46 Academic settings
54 They're likely to come to blows
55 1964 Hitchcock thriller
56 Channel surfer's locale, maybe
57 __ Indian
58 Superfluities

DOWN

1 Make a bundle
2 Intestinal parts
3 Wrangle
4 Lady's man
5 Only same-year N.C.A.A. and N.I.T. tourney winner (1950)
6 Piece of cake?
7 French wave
8 Despicable
9 About 1.3 cubic yards
10 Engaging individual
11 Pervasive quality
12 Place for a pin
13 Incessantly

14 Standard bearers
18 "It Must Be __"
21 "The Carpetbaggers" co-star, 1964
22 Sure target
23 Bond, but not James Bond
24 They're called on account of rain
25 Troubles
26 Shade of red
27 "And what __ rare as . . ."
29 Precollege
30 Fought
31 Peak near Paterno
32 Clip-and-file item
33 Community event

34 Treat with milk
35 Stack part
39 No-goodnik
40 Suitable for extreme dieters
41 Sound beginning?
42 Buckwheat pancakes
43 "Mighty Lak' a Rose" composer
44 Architectural moldings
45 Unspecified no.
47 One of the sisters in "Sisters"
48 Year in the reign of Edward I
49 Blanch

50 French part of the U.S.A.
51 Offspring
52 A really big shoe
53 C.I.S. members, once

by Bob Klahn   Friday, November 6, 1998

30

SHORTZ SAYS:
A slight spoiler here, but something you should know: A pangram is a piece of writing that contains all the letters of the alphabet at least once. Matt Gaffney creates crosswords for the online magazine Slate.

ACROSS

1 Hardly an Oscar candidate
4 Worksite tool
7 Singer
13 Medical suffix
14 In __ (stuck)
16 Muddy
17 Popular side dish
19 Canadian writer Robertson __
20 Walton who wrote "The Compleat Angler"
21 Tell (from)
23 Kind of wire
24 Send, in a way
25 BASIC command
29 Commercial stuff: Abbr.
30 Settles
31 Bumpkin
32 Yuletide décor
33 Turned bad
34 This crossword grid, when completed correctly
37 Trips
38 Ristorante offering
39 Interstate info
40 Plasters, e.g.
41 Day in Granada
44 Team data
45 Angola's Savimbi
46 Winter warmer
47 U.S. Open champ, 1985–87
48 Ending with two-, three-, four-, etc.
49 Henry Clay, e.g.
53 Short-term solution
55 Bring back
56 Stereotyped Beverly Hills resident
57 Big shooter
58 Spanish novelist Blasco __
59 Kind of wire
60 Expanse

DOWN

1 Like some pigeons
2 In shock
3 Noisy talkers
4 "Listen!"
5 Spanish eye
6 Steel in writing
7 Ancient book
8 On __ with
9 Part of U.S.N.A.: Abbr.
10 Pollution meas.
11 Wish undone
12 Hoped-for reply
15 What I, the constructor, had to do while making this puzzle
18 __ in apple
22 City NE of Casablanca
24 Honeymoon destination, with "the"
25 Primitive "drum"
26 Some pods
27 Overflow
28 Worn
30 Egyptian believers
31 Meditators
32 Suggests
33 High-hats
34 It has a bill of fare
35 Bankruptcy
36 It's breathtaking
37 Wandering __ (houseplant)
40 Slip on
41 Dork
42 Charge
43 Inability to read
45 Spanish wine town
46 Cookware item
47 Troubadour's subject
48 National frozen dessert chain
49 "It must be him, __ . . ." (60's lyric)
50 Johnny __
51 Gardner of film
52 Food holder
54 Paper in a pot

by Matt Gaffney   Saturday, November 14, 1998

SHORTZ SAYS:

This elegant construction is built around a humorous quotation running across three lines of the grid. When you're finished, the circled letters, in order (reading left to right, line by line), will give you the name of the quip's author.

ACROSS

1 Open-mouthed
6 Jacket part
10 Den
14 Allied
15 + or −
16 Riding the waves
17 Coin of Stockholm
18 __ impasse
19 Hunting target
20 Part 1 of a quip by the writer named in the circled letters
23 Born
24 No longer secret
25 1950's White House name
27 "Jeopardy!" host
30 Place to view a Goya
31 Is responsible for
35 Midmorning
36 Part 2 of the quip
41 "Alice" waitress
42 First in a line of cars
43 Sprites
46 Bordering
50 Actress Dianne
51 Balm ingredient
54 "__ the ramparts . . ."
55 End of the quip
59 All there
60 In olden times
61 River through Switzerland
62 Adenauer nickname, with "Der"
63 Film director Peter
64 Put into the ground
65 Grab, slangily
66 Former spouses
67 Gadabouts

DOWN

1 Obliquely
2 Steel beam
3 Actress Renée
4 Former Transportation Secretary Federico

5 Dutch cheese
6 "Star Trek" setting
7 __ Dame
8 Acteur Delon
9 Shut (up)
10 Daytona 500 organization
11 Body shop figure
12 Shores
13 Cry before "You're it!"
21 Crookedly
22 Mischief-maker
26 Centuries and centuries
28 Troop grp.
29 Poetic contraction
32 Library sound

33 Italy's bottom
34 Ending with pay
36 Generally
37 Approach, as the next item of business
38 Fish-eating eagles
39 Enzyme suffix
40 Bother
41 Small number
44 Respect
45 Actor Erwin
47 This evenin'
48 High schooler
49 They may be marching
51 Not the main building
52 One of the Arnazes

53 Humdingers
56 T. __ Price of finance
57 Math course
58 "Oops!"
59 Wane

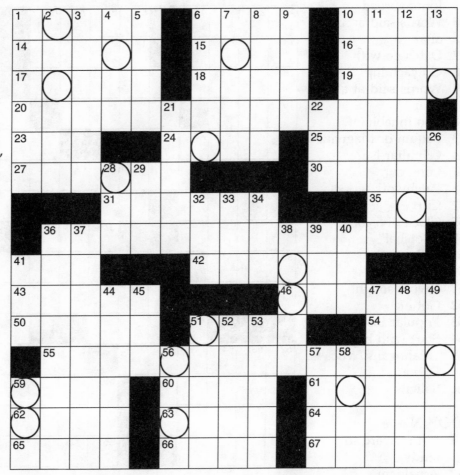

by Glenn E. Sykes

Wednesday, February 3, 1999

32

SHORTZ SAYS:
A particular thing—common to almost all crosswords (and almost all writing of any sort)—is wholly missing in this crossword. What is it?

ACROSS
1 Daddy
5 "Now!" in a hospital
9 Points
13 King of Norway
14 Mountain lion
15 It follows larval
16 Cunning
18 Of any amount
19 Chit
20 Music and painting, for two
21 Drinks in big amounts
22 Author's assistant
24 Spinning toys
25 Quick-thinking
31 Cain was his son
34 Thin
35 John, abroad
36 Words said at an altar
37 Dah's go-with
38 Go yachting
39 Words said at an altar
40 Zoo inhabitant
43 Paquin or Magnani
44 Gibraltar-ish?
47 Long cut
48 Patchwork works
52 Curt
55 Clock division
57 "Gotcha!"
58 Balloon
59 Chubby plus
61 Favors sought
62 Got off
63 Popular insulator
64 Start with boy or girl
65 "Mahogany" vocalist Diana
66 Solicits

DOWN
1 Put forward for study
2 Amalgam
3 Fulfill an obligation
4 "Mogambo" star, familiarly
5 Lacking luxury and comfort
6 Bunch of hairs
7 Famous __
8 Word with withholding
9 Musician of old
10 It's found in a ring
11 Summon
12 Harms
15 Shrub with a tasty fruit
17 Door part
21 Middling
23 Philosophical holdings
24 Tooth buildup
26 Bit in a salad bar
27 __ donna
28 Comic King
29 Half-dollar, say
30 Kind of nut
31 Company with cars
32 Dummy
33 Army no-show
38 Alias of H. H. Munro
40 Conforms
41 Cartoonist Thomas
42 Asian fruits
45 Common lizard
46 Junkyard dogs
49 __ lazuli
50 Not too brainy
51 Historical writings
52 "S.O.S." pop group
53 Rorschach stain
54 Applaud (for)
55 Luminous ring
56 Football's __ Armstrong
59 __ and away
60 Dr.'s org.

by Gayle Dean

Tuesday, May 4, 1999

Zack Butler was just 24 years old, studying robotics at Carnegie Mellon University in Pittsburgh, when he created this elegant crossword for The Times. A wunderkind of sorts, Zack has won several prizes at the annual World Puzzle Championship, which means that he's as good at solving puzzles as he is at making them.

ACROSS

1 BA or AF plane
4 Better
9 Play for time
14 Gobbled up
15 Love, Neapolitan-style
16 Charged
17 Event where the twist was done
18 Start of a quote by Rep. Mo Udall, 1990, regarding the Presidency
20 Quote, part 2
22 Ready for action
23 Kids' book character Amelia __
25 The first X?
26 Trail
29 Gets warmer, perhaps
31 Elvis's birthplace
33 Class with dissections: Abbr.
36 Transmission component
38 Quote, part 3
39 Quote, part 4
42 Quote, part 5
43 Mother of Apollo
44 Center
45 Certain contracts
47 Kind of bar
49 Certain addition
50 "Eureka!"
52 Stage, as a historical drama
56 Kind of band
58 Quote, part 6
59 End of the quote
63 W.C.
64 Leonardo da __
65 Feel
66 Disputed psych. phenomenon
67 Altair or Sirius, astronomically speaking

68 Singer Bob
69 "Absolutely!"

DOWN

1 Indian term of respect
2 Vermont resort
3 Lukewarm
4 Silken fabric
5 Org. much in economic news
6 One of a kind
7 Switch ending
8 Send in
9 Relaxing job
10 Woodland creature
11 Tunnel builder
12 Golf ball position

13 Digital watch feature: Abbr.
19 "Who __?"
21 Soup ingredients
24 Enemy of the Moor
26 Slower than adagio
27 Rehem
28 Former Philadelphia Mayor Wilson
30 Items with dials
32 "Turandot" composer
33 See 51-Down
34 Banister's end
35 Perpendicular to radial
37 Backtracking

40 Kind of act passed in 1970
41 Fall (to)
46 Remove
48 Big name in magazine publishing
51 Equivalent of 33-Down?
53 "Gang aft __": Burns
54 Selected
55 Pseudo-convertibles
56 A whale of a menace
57 Fit to __
59 One of the Gabors
60 Greek letters
61 Atlanta-based station
62 Sugar suffix

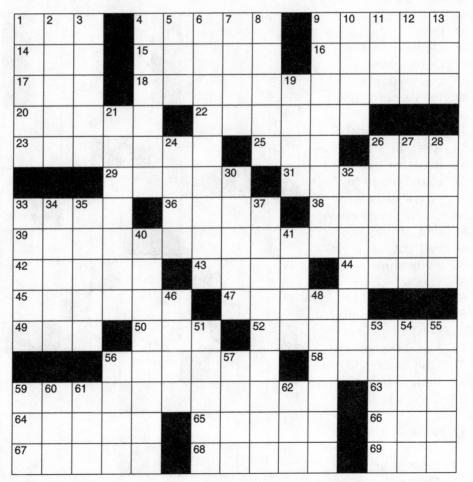

by Zack Butler

Thursday, May 20, 1999

(34)

ACROSS

1 Railroad siding
5 Israeli author ___ Oz
9 Boxer's nickname
14 Cellar contents
15 Judah's mother
16 Woman's name meaning "loved"
17 See 5-Down
18 Mezzo's colleague
19 Closes in on
20 Start of a quote by Booker T. Washington
23 Clear
24 Reverses a dele
25 Oktoberfest souvenir
27 Dinosaur trapper
30 Half an LP
34 Mitigates
39 Does a butler's job
40 Quote, part 3
41 Quote, part 4
43 Quote, part 5
44 1993 accord signer
46 Quagmires
48 Highly influential
50 Alter, in a way
51 Raingear brand
53 Introduction to physics
58 C.I.A.'s predecessor
61 End of the quote
64 Fall guy
66 Conked out
67 Speck
68 Over
69 Modern pentathlon need
70 Joie de vivre
71 1944 battle site
72 Johnny Bench's team
73 Lucie's brother

DOWN

1 Influences
2 Kitchen light
3 Excessive
4 Change chemically
5 With 17-Across, Hawkeye Pierce portrayer
6 Get all mushy
7 Blue language
8 Photographers' gigs
9 Dr. Pangloss's pupil, in Voltaire
10 Make haste
11 Quote, part 2
12 Unimportant
13 Nudnik
21 Early movie dog
22 Workaholic's lack
26 Cries out for
28 Kin of vivace
29 Striped shirt wearer
31 Chicano bears?

32 Five after four
33 Tolkien forest creatures
34 Actress Rehan and others
35 Ticked off
36 Emulated Janet Evans
37 Not suitable
38 Prefix meaning "with"
42 Expression of excitement
45 Painkiller
47 Latin trio member?
49 More salacious
52 Sandpiper's cousin
54 Recoiled

55 Oarlock
56 Rudner and Moreno
57 Muscat native
58 Iridescent stone
59 Stuffing herb
60 Quote, part 6
62 Herbicide's target
63 Time to beware
65 Obedience school command

by Alan Olschwang

Wednesday, June 23, 1999

SHORTZ SAYS:

When I appeared on "Martha Stewart Living" in June 2000, I brought this puzzle with me to demonstrate how crosswords are constructed. Martha was fascinated by the art and precision of crossword construction, and I knew that the humor of the answers here would make her and her audience laugh.

35

ACROSS

1 City where "Phantom of the Opera" is set
6 Langley, for one: Abbr.
9 Where to put a pin on a jacket
14 By oneself
15 Ripken of the Orioles
16 Furious
17 "Come on, ducks, it's time to start!"
20 Clothes lines
21 A or B, on a record
22 ___-tse
23 Court dividers
25 Royal heirs
27 "Down with the glue factory proposal!"
31 1999 combatants
35 A Gershwin
36 Head, to Henri
37 Ancient city north of Jerusalem
38 Take the show on the road
40 Reagan Attorney General Edwin
42 Kind of bean
43 Historical records
45 Close
47 Tues. preceder
48 Make-a-million game
49 "Phooey! It's shearing time again!"
51 Up to speed
53 Late-night host Jay
54 Nabokov novel
57 Lady's man
59 Highway exits
62 "I need instructions on catching mice!"
66 Flood protector
67 Earl Grey, e.g.
68 Alternative to "window"
69 Step
70 1492 and 2001: Abbr.
71 Tibetan legends

DOWN

1 Chum
2 Pub brews
3 Uncreative education
4 Crazy
5 Part
6 Play a role
7 Queries on the Internet
8 Somewhat sky-colored
9 Permit
10 Biblical vessel
11 Kid's beach toy
12 Sicilian volcano
13 Toy building block
18 Holds in high regard
19 Hubbub
24 Place
26 Studio stages
27 Critically important
28 Maine university town
29 Ridicule
30 Actress Davis
32 Skewed square
33 "It Had to ___"
34 Breezy talk
37 Do something courageous
39 Pro ___
41 Circus performer
44 Washington arm-bender
46 Escape
49 Pageant winner
50 Hollywood bio "___ Dearest"
52 Durocher or DiCaprio
54 Pointed tools
55 Eating regimen
56 Thomas ___ Edison
58 Addict
60 Nuisance
61 Songs for one
63 Flower garland
64 Possesses
65 "A Nightmare on Elm Street" creator Craven

by Stephanie Spadaccini   Monday, August 2, 1999

36

SHORTZ SAYS:
If I even hint at this puzzle's ingenious theme, I'll spoil your pleasure in figuring it out. All I'll say is that 33-Across contains a hint, and 7-Down, brilliantly, provides an additional clue.

ACROSS

1 Lookout point
5 Car protector
8 Candidate for a psych ward
13 Memorable 1989 hurricane
14 One makes one Trigger happy
15 Grosset's partner in publishing
16 Jungle creature
18 Delineate again
19 __ boy
20 Meantime
22 Chapter 11 filers
23 Wise
26 "You are too" response
27 Some workers
28 NATO refusal
29 Dict. listing
30 Ex-Bosoxer Petrocelli
31 It may be hard for one person to carry
33 Hint to filling in four squares in this puzzle
35 Popular Tonka toys
38 Time and time again
39 Greetings
42 Brown hue
43 Cut __
44 Summer treat
45 Old dental supply
48 Pioneer in Surrealism
49 Go over again
50 Smock
51 Early explorer of Florida
53 How things are seen
55 Relatives of Siberians
56 Norma Webster's middle name
57 Uphold
58 Squalid
59 Place that's 58-Across
60 European tongue

DOWN

1 Soft leather
2 Flee
3 Trojan War chief
4 Racer
5 French word of approval
6 Glow
7 People good at making connections
8 Court figures
9 Violating orders
10 Hillary, for one
11 Mo. neighbor
12 Unseal
15 German number
17 W.W. II org.
21 Sets
24 Become prone
25 Suffix with insist
27 Isn't doing well
30 Part of A.A.R.P.: Abbr.
31 Lay
32 Lt.'s inferior
33 Bravely endure
34 Declawed manx, e.g.
35 Coalesce
36 Mozart's "L'__ del Cairo"
37 Bouncer type
39 Medal giver
40 Where to find pitchers?
41 Do printer's work
43 Muslim title
44 Seafood delicacy
46 All meshed up?
47 __ point (certain stitch)
48 Wing
51 Pop
52 __ Lilly & Co.
54 180 degree turn, in slang

by Robert H. Wolfe

Thursday, August 12, 1999

SHORTZ SAYS:
The basic format of crossword puzzles seems endlessly adaptable, as illustrated once more here. The grid features a three-part riddle, the answer to which can be found by rearranging the letters in the 10 circled squares.

ACROSS

1 False "handle"
6 Tag along
10 Window-__
14 Freetown currency unit
15 Western Samoa's capital
16 Go in the water just a little way
17 __ good faith
18 Carry on
19 Confess openly
20 Start of a question
23 Found a new tenant for
24 "What's more . . ."
25 Arid expanse
28 Wood furniture worker
32 Bio bit
33 "Animal House" house
36 The Donald's first ex
37 Engine sounds
40 Middle of the question
41 Splits apart
42 Square (with)
43 Doctrines
45 Top off
46 Odd-shaped figure
48 Sports surprises
51 Rarer than rare
52 Nouveau __
54 End of the question (Rearrange the circled letters for the answer)
61 N.Y.S.E. competitor
62 Seaside bird
63 Alamogordo's county
64 In the 50's or 60's, say
65 "I did it!"
66 Unearthly
67 Hoover hookup
68 Charon's river
69 "Oui" and "si"

DOWN

1 What there oughta be
2 Poland's Walesa
3 Scintilla
4 "Peer Gynt" dancer
5 Fax originator
6 __ diem
7 Eyeball benders
8 Tiny car
9 Bothers incessantly
10 Graceful pool entrance
11 Moneyed one
12 Meaning of wavy lines, in the comics
13 Seats with kneelers
21 Norway's patron saint
22 Studio sign
25 See-through wrap
26 Suffix on bygone nightclub names
27 "Sunset Boulevard" Tony winner George
28 Florist's cutting
29 "Eraserhead" star Jack
30 "This foolishness must __ once!"
31 Coarse tools
34 Completely botch
35 Fool
38 Differential gear's spot
39 George of "Just Shoot Me"
44 So great
47 Wise kids?
49 "Rats!"
50 Soft seat
52 Lecherous
53 Mountaineer's tool
54 Dash gauge
55 Melville novel
56 Boardroom V.I.P.'s
57 Part of Q.E.D.
58 Half a matched set
59 Put-in-Bay's lake
60 Fictitious Richard et al.

by Thomas W. Schier
Wednesday, September 15, 1999

38

SHORTZ SAYS:
Fifty-five of this puzzle's 185 letters—almost 30% of the entire construction—are part of the theme. Quite a nice and original theme, too.

ACROSS

1 States
6 Lawyers make it
10 Quarrel
14 Kosher
15 Last word in the New Testament
16 Olio
17 See 22-Down
19 Old Phillips 66 rival
20 All over the counter, say
21 Sacred place
22 Elizabethan pronoun
25 See 22-Down
28 Chips in
30 Sphere
31 "Norma __"
32 Meathead's father-in-law
36 Like a very rare day in hell
40 Victorian __
41 See 22-Down
43 Eng. defender
44 Sicilian spouter
46 Oil city of west Texas
47 "__ my brother's keeper?"
48 Florida's Miami-__ County
50 Swimming pool site, sometimes
52 See 22-Down
57 Salon job
58 Search blindly
59 Cleo of jazz
61 "__ it the truth!"
62 See 22-Down
67 Dirty
68 "Bye!"
69 Ruth's mother-in-law
70 Entreat
71 Goes on TV
72 "__ Fell Out of Heaven" (1936 hit)

DOWN

1 Totality
2 Neck design
3 It may be coddled
4 Hastily puts together
5 __ aerobics
6 Monte __
7 Valuable violin
8 Jiffy
9 From Okla. City to Tulsa
10 Finish, of a sort
11 Ziti or orzo
12 Examine
13 Thunderous one?
18 Chip's partner
21 Simian
22 Word that precedes six other answers in this puzzle
23 The Tin Woodsman's quest
24 City on the Allegheny River
26 Manicurists' jobs
27 Walnuts and others
29 Dated
33 __ Island Red
34 Gives up
35 Part of a giggle
37 Speak
38 Not so believable
39 See 22-Down
42 Hit hard
45 With skill
49 Sampras specialty
51 Met production responsibilities?
52 Rap sheet listing
53 Aegean region
54 Opposite of radial
55 Villainous Shakespearean roles
56 Spasm
58 Exhibit shock
60 Ship of Columbus
62 Big TV maker
63 Sequel's sequel
64 Camp sight
65 Actress Thurman
66 What to call a baronet

by Chris Sallade

Wednesday, October 27, 1999

SHORTZ SAYS:
For most constructors, creating a grid in which every letter forms part of two words (across and down) is challenging enough. This puzzle has answers running through the two long diagonals as well. The puzzle's two authors have never met; they collaborated on this entirely by e-mail.

ACROSS

1 "The Lost Weekend" subject
4 Scream
8 Care provider, to a child
14 Crater feature
15 "This one's __"
16 Land on Lake Victoria
17 "The __ Daba Honeymoon"
18 Booty location
20 Microfiche
22 Dance in Dublin
23 Candle material
24 Runway walker
27 Nastiness
30 Eggnog topper
33 Pedro's affirmative
36 Sawyer of ABC
38 Ryan's "Love Story" co-star
39 Post-E.R. place
40 X marks it
42 Laid up
43 Race unit
44 Gossipy Hopper
45 Eskimo's need
46 Go a long way
48 __ the Jebusite, of I and II Chronicles
51 Muscat moola
53 Saws
57 Like pocket dicts.
58 Fall guy
61 What this puzzle is
64 It may have a silver lining
65 Some sorority women
66 Merry-go-round music
67 Key locale: Abbr.
68 Bars
69 Apollo vehicles
70 A Chaplin

DOWN

1 Early writing
2 Legbone
3 Like some talk
4 Revolver, in old slang
5 Hocked
6 Gen. Bradley
7 Care for
8 Xis' predecessors
9 "Gross!"
10 Aircraft engine
11 Nonelectronic correspondence
12 "Got it"
13 Ending with Ecuador
19 School of thought
21 Year in Edward the Confessor's reign
25 __ account (never)
26 Tuneful twosome
28 Had too much, briefly
29 Bungle
31 Fashion mag
32 Richly adorn
33 Bank deposit
34 Cupcake topper
35 Sweet vegetable
37 On __ with
40 "__-Team"
41 Hot spot
45 Hose hole
47 Shrew
49 Incendiary stuff
50 Whizzes
52 Ukr., e.g., once
54 Slips
55 Like an eager guest, maybe
56 Position
57 Embracers
59 Pen part
60 Gallic girlfriend
61 Stocking part
62 Easy mark
63 __ Missouri

DIAGONAL

1 Pirate booty
68 More pirate booty

by Bill Zais and Nancy Salomon   Wednesday, December 1, 1999

40

SHORTZ SAYS:
The longest theme answers in a crossword usually run horizontally. In this puzzle they run vertically, for a reason.

ACROSS

1 Graphic __
5 No-frills
10 Deer sir
14 Something eaten with the palms?
15 Exxon alternative
16 Quaint sigh
17 About
18 Red Sea borderer
19 Charger's acquisition
20 Dickens's pen name
21 Fine-tune
22 C&W singer Tritt
24 Home of the legendary Morgan le Fay
26 They're involved in pageantry
28 Admonition to a child
29 Fortune 500 chemicals company
30 Like Beethoven's Sonata No. 30
31 Commedia dell'__
32 Helping for a while, with "over"
34 Sheraton hotels owner
35 Be busy
37 One of the Chaplins
38 Phys., e.g.
40 Honest __
42 They're cast
45 "How the Other Half Lives" author Jacob
48 Singing syllable
49 Honeybun
50 "Seinfeld" regular
52 Source of some clicking
54 More crafty
55 Extremely
56 Off-course
58 Journalist Kupcinet
59 Note
60 Big name in daytime TV

62 Cash in Capua
63 __ B
64 Heads-up
65 Quotation notation
66 Actress Daly
67 Hot spot
68 Ernie's "Sesame Street" pal

DOWN

1 "Open sesame!" sayer
2 Exceed
3 Jungle swinger
4 "So __ me!"
5 Rifle attachment
6 End of grace
7 With 11-Down, 3-Down's last words?
8 Rocks
9 Hold in check
10 Begin's co-Nobelist
11 See 7-Down
12 Completely surrounding
13 Prepares
21 Ad __
23 Steps up?
25 Stead
27 Say "Li'l Abner," say
33 Violinist Stern
36 Goldfinger?
39 Rugged rock
40 Crack
41 With pluck

43 Holiday window item
44 What tellers lack?
46 Mistaken
47 Leporello, e.g., in "Don Giovanni"
51 Put
53 Stingless bee
57 Certain money transfer
61 Schnozz tip?
62 Family dog, for short

by Harvey Estes and Nancy Salomon   **Thursday, December 16, 1999**

SHORTZ SAYS:
Four 15-letter answers reading across, and two more 15-letter answers going down—it's a seemingly impossible grid to fill. Yet Manny Nosowsky makes the task look easy, using familiar vocabulary that's unusual and colorful at the same time.

ACROSS

1 Six French kings
8 Cheese dish
15 Had 100 or more
17 One stirring up trouble for management
18 Darts
19 City on the Aire
20 "Grand Ole Opry" airer
21 Philosophy subjects
22 Level
23 Glen Gray & the Casa __ Orchestra
24 __ Fail (Irish coronation stone)
25 House coat
26 "Le Fifre" artist
27 Becomes twisted
29 One of the Andrews Sisters
30 Breathless
31 Howled
32 Whence the line "The meek shall inherit the earth"
34 Elbows on the table
37 Way to get a job
38 Regular and long
39 Seasonal serving
40 Like some muscles
41 Aquino's successor in the Philippines
42 "Count __"
43 Wanted letters
44 Prefix with tropic
45 Prop in a Wild West show
46 Noted storyteller
49 "Don't rush me!"
50 They may be half or full
51 Like elbows, sometimes

DOWN

1 There's one on most coins
2 Arrests
3 Slips and such
4 Holds up
5 Reply to "That a fact?"
6 __ Xing
7 Ranker
8 College leader
9 Take for __
10 So-and-sos
11 In-flight announcement, for short
12 Stopped talking
13 Tireless ones
14 Like poison ivy leaves
16 Winners get them
22 Philately collection
23 Not so tough
25 Shorty: Var.
26 Noted pyramid builders
28 Beaver's nearest relative
29 Big clubs
31 Antitank weapons
32 Perfect role model
33 Washington address
34 Charades, basically
35 Rotten
36 Glossed over
38 Places of art
41 Copal or mastic
42 Mediterranean tourist destination
44 Sunshine Biscuits brand
45 Pseudologist
47 They may be civil: Abbr.
48 And that's not all

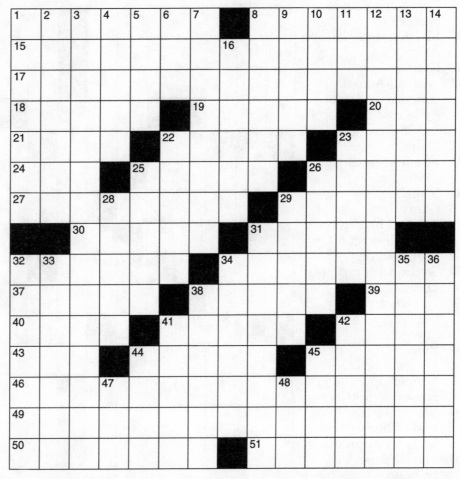

by Manny Nosowsky

Friday, January 7, 2000

42

SHORTZ SAYS:
Another Manny Nosowsky tour de force, this puzzle features three sets of theme answers.
Look carefully—there is a reason for the italicized word in each theme clue.

ACROSS

1 Get rid of
8 Loser
15 City on Lake Ontario
16 "Well, I __!"
17 With 18-Across, Spendthrift's motto (which cracks *me* up!)
18 See 17-Across
19 W.W. II combat area: Abbr.
20 Lender's recourse
22 Military mission
23 Stage assistant's job
25 Phnom __
26 Goldman __ (brokerage)
29 Noggin
31 Latin lover's word
34 They keep people off beaches
36 Khartoum-to-Nairobi dir.
37 Gray
38 With 40-Across, American novelist (who cracks *me* up!)
40 See 38-Across
42 Staffs
43 Neediest cases site?: Abbr.
45 Swinging
46 Gamy
47 It might be involved in a police roundup
49 Beer delivery
50 Settles with certainty
52 Lore
54 "__ what you say, but . . ."
56 Sludge
57 Break
60 With 62-Across, Runner-up (who cracks *me* up!)
62 See 60-Across
65 End-of-book matter
66 Major coca producer
67 Spouse's meek response
68 Unity

DOWN

1 Suit to __
2 Tug, say
3 Estimator's phrase
4 "The Thin Man" co-star
5 Business letters?
6 Popular vodka, familiarly
7 Zeroing (in on)
8 Yemeni city
9 Linda __, Supergirl's alias
10 One way to run
11 Novelist Tillie
12 "Unchain My Heart" singer
13 Ship to Colchis
14 Brightly-colored
21 Prima donna problems
23 Buddies
24 Packinghouse stamp
25 Procter & Gamble brand
26 Jerk
27 Shake like __
28 Crows' hangouts
30 It may be temporary or practical
32 Director Louis
33 Follows
35 Shows of irritation
37 Stars on stage
39 AT&T competitor
41 Gambling, e.g.
44 "Do __ others . . ."
47 Pacific
48 Park feature
51 Surrendered, with "in"
53 Enticed
54 Words to an "old chap"
55 Harbor
56 Actor Sharif
57 "__ Me a Break" (title for this puzzle?)
58 Sales term
59 Grps. that liaise with principals
61 Dietary abbr.
63 Order at the Green Dragon
64 China's __ Piao

by Manny Nosowsky   **Thursday, February 10, 2000**

SHORTZ SAYS:

Note the date of this puzzle (April 1), which is significant. Solvers on The New York Times's online crossword forum voted this one of their favorite crosswords of the year.

ACROSS

1 Torment
5 Some socials
9 Golfers' needs
14 Over yonder
15 Joyous cry
16 "Are you in __?"
17 Little one
18 Utah Lake is to its west
19 Tarnish
20 Counterfeiters' nemeses
21 Rocket launcher
22 Marina site
23 Ministers
25 List for a new hire
27 Squish, squash or squelch
29 "You're lookin' at your person!"
33 Have words with
37 Start of a newsgroup name online
38 Orient
39 Attempts
42 Measurer
43 North Korea's __ Il Sung
44 Breadth
45 Cooking meas.
46 Really here
48 "What fools these mortals be" writer
50 Beacon
55 Half-sister of Absalom
58 Pen mothers
60 Nair rival
61 Formulaic
62 Littermates
63 Camus's "L'__ de siège"
64 Officer's jacket
65 Something copied: Abbr.
66 Countertenor, maybe
67 Musical notes
68 Rib
69 Sri Lankan exports

DOWN

1 Flirt
2 Bouquet garni element
3 Conned
4 Graph line indication
5 Fund-raising suffix
6 Tongue-lashing
7 High branch
8 Paste makers
9 "Sophie, __ and Belle" (1996 musical)
10 Here today, gone tomorrow
11 Hard work
12 Air
13 Informal tops
24 Loud streakers
26 Rulers have them
28 Absorbed
30 Synthetic
31 "My life __ open book"
32 Plumbing joints
33 Angers, with "off"
34 __ League
35 kissers
36 Perseveres
40 Part of a Yarborough, maybe, in bridge
41 Jump in the Winter Olympics
47 Log-cutting area
49 Standing
51 Oafish
52 Imply
53 Inside pump
54 Certain crosses
55 Timeout signs
56 In __ (stagnant)
57 Make money
59 Certain N.C.O.

by Manny Nosowsky

Saturday, April 1, 2000

SHORTZ SAYS:

Peter Gordon created this puzzle as a sly announcement that he and his wife were expecting. Daughter Phoebe was born on October 28, 2000. Peter also has the distinction of having the first Sunday crossword published under my editorship—one in which the seven colors of the spectrum (red, orange, yellow, green, blue, indigo and violet) had to be colored in the grid.

44

ACROSS

1 Woody's "Scenes From a Mall" co-star
6 Manx of the house?
9 "Yes, __"
13 Bucolic
14 Leave breathless
15 "__ la vista, baby"
16 Susan Lucci's Emmy-winning soap role
17 Superman foe
19 1992 U.S. Open golf champion
21 Like some stores of old
22 The Untouchables' leader
24 Named yet unnamed
25 Fished
29 Bread in the oven
31 Tub with a whirlpool
34 Sans-__ type
35 The silent brother
36 Fancy calculator button
37 John Philip Sousa, after a pregnant pause?
40 Poetic preposition
41 Fedora parts
42 Down time
43 Triathlon part
44 Steak order
45 Pain soother
46 Strong joe
47 Line on a map
49 Opens
53 Still fresh
58 March of Time presentations
60 Shylock's doing
61 Dog in "Blondie"
62 Snapper trapper
63 City in northern France
64 Wild revelry
65 Hairstyles
66 Certain locks

DOWN

1 Cy Young winner Saberhagen
2 New money
3 Fit
4 Sail a zigzag course
5 "Ishtar" director, after a pregnant pause?
6 Loses color
7 "You," in a rebus puzzle
8 College book
9 Part of a book?
10 "A Hard Road to Glory" author
11 Lots
12 K follower
15 With "The," Tom Clancy novel, after a pregnant pause?
18 Delaware Indian
20 Turner of TV channels
23 Clink
25 Disk-shaped flower
26 1940's–60's Indian P.M.
27 Inexperienced
28 Jar part
30 Globes
31 Smart
32 Stuffed animal at a carnival
33 Ticked off
35 __ to the throne
38 Grave's counterpart
39 Okla. neighbor
45 Proscribe
46 Slovenly
48 Gives the boot
49 Word processing command
50 Approach
51 Gulp of liquor
52 Enrapture
54 China setting
55 Like dishwater
56 Creator of Perry and Della
57 Batiking needs
59 Many an August birth

by Peter Gordon

Wednesday, April 12, 2000

SHORTZ SAYS:

Most puzzle solvers are familiar with the word ladder, in which, for example, COLD can be converted to WARM by changing one letter at a time, making a new word at each step (COLD, CORD, WORD, WARD, WARM). Greg Staples is the first constructor I'm aware of who ever incorporated a word ladder into a crossword theme. The 10 unclued answers in this puzzle (from 20- to 57-Across) show how he did it.

ACROSS

1 Kind of tent
4 Strong criticism
8 Ages
14 Charlotte-to-Raleigh dir.
15 Parks in 1955 news
16 "Big deal"
17 With skill
19 __ Club
20 *Start of the word ladder
21 *Second step
23 *Third step
24 Polite guest
27 Denver clock setting: Abbr.
28 Smart set
31 Communicate successfully
34 Jackie's second
35 *Fourth step
37 *Fifth step
38 Whines
40 Take care (of)
43 *Sixth step
44 *Seventh step
45 "O patria __" ("Aida" aria)
46 Perfect hits
49 Happening
51 Duke Ellington's "__ Got Me"
52 Pay back
54 *Eighth step
56 *Ninth step
57 *End of the word ladder
61 Censors' signs
64 Brainiac
66 Stands for things
67 Put on board
68 Grazing ground
69 Saddam Hussein, e.g.
70 Chapeau's spot
71 A little work

DOWN

1 They can be sweet
2 Word processor command
3 Amazon's source
4 When "Dallas" aired: Abbr.
5 "__ luck!"
6 Provided that
7 Olympic water sports competitor
8 Tee preceder
9 Luau serving
10 Has a tab
11 Gene carrier
12 Ride, so to speak
13 Some may be false
18 Chooses
22 Fido or Fluffy
25 __ corpus
26 1994 Peace Nobelist
28 Fifth of 12
29 Baseball card stat.
30 One of Jack's qualities
32 Baby
33 Shoot the breeze
36 Canadian skater Brian
39 N.L. Central team, on a scoreboard
40 Sever
41 Fall from grace
42 "Dig in!"
44 Legal legacy
46 Like a baby in a highchair
47 Throat flaps
48 Hankering
50 Blow off steam
53 "A house __ a home"
55 Trickle
58 Congo river
59 Bleacher feature
60 Unforeseen difficulty
62 Arafat's grp.
63 Jet-set jet
65 Nor. neighbor

by Greg Staples

Thursday, April 27, 2000

46

ACROSS

1 Water collector
5 Even a bit
10 Battleground of July 1944
14 Winged
15 The sixth part of 7-Down
16 Shade of blue
17 About
18 See 22-Across
20 Child's need, maybe
22 Part of an American plan, at a hotel
23 Examine
24 No-no's opposite?
26 Closed
29 Patty Hearst's name in the S.L.A.
34 Conclusive
37 See 34-Across
39 Jai __
40 San __, Calif.
41 Suffix with my-
42 See 44-Across
44 Member of a crew
45 Part of a script
46 "Bewitched" role
48 Source
50 Writers' org.
54 Pits
57 11 p.m., for some
59 See 54-Across
62 "Fort Apache" actor, 1948
63 Dover specialty
64 Ticket category
65 British poet laureate Nahum
66 Made like
67 Exalted
68 Discordia's Greek counterpart

DOWN

1 "You __ mouthful!"
2 Arm twisters?
3 St. __ College, in Indiana
4 Sensible step
5 Like some doors
6 Surfing site, with "the"
7 2000, e.g., in Spain
8 Actress Ullmann
9 "Marshall __ Money Guide"
10 Portico
11 Spree
12 Cooking aid
13 Previously heard
19 "Otello" librettist
21 Author Rand
24 Sailor's aid
25 Mean
27 "The joke's __"
28 Female with a showy mate
30 Hawaii
31 Big auto parts company
32 "The doctor __"
33 Slightly
34 Handsome dogs, informally
35 "Smart" one
36 Out of reach
38 Uproar
43 Have a connection (to)
47 Fine, slangily
49 Ottoman Empire founder
51 Obsolescent carnival prize
52 Treasured instrument
53 Netanyahu's predecessor
54 Alphabet run
55 Unused
56 Straits
57 Bicycle adjunct
58 Isabella d'__
59 Traditional Olympics basketball powerhouse
60 Committed reply
61 Gist

by Richard Hughes   **Thursday, May 4, 2000**

SHORTZ SAYS:
As I mentioned earlier, a daily crossword with 72 or fewer answers doesn't need a theme. Yet this 70-word puzzle has seven (count 'em!) theme answers, and a beautiful interlock besides. Patrick Berry is one of just a few people in the country who earns his living by constructing crosswords. If he keeps up quality like this, he won't ever have to worry about how to pay the rent.

47

ACROSS

1 Arthur of 70's–80's TV
4 Most uncomfortable, as weather
10 Burning
13 Last page
14 Provincial ruler in the Byzantine Empire
15 Like old records
16 Home of "The Sopranos"
17 Person with a hat, maybe
18 He beat Connors to win Wimbledon
19 "When __ said and done . . ."
21 Business tycoon's problem?
23 Landlord's problem?
26 Sink
27 Fire-breathing monster
29 Begrudges
30 Casino worker's problem?
32 Title acquired in church, maybe
33 Soda jerk's problem?
38 Whistle blower
39 Shopper's problem?
40 Modern treaty subjects
44 Like some messages
47 Dolt
49 War minister's problem?
51 Sweepstakes entrant's problem?
53 100 centesimos
54 Detachment of soldiers
55 More repulsive
58 Vinaigrette ingredient
59 Uses a sewing shuttle
60 Café __ (laced coffee)
61 Swiss canton
62 Arch
63 Lens cover?
64 Sen. Stevens of Alaska

DOWN

1 "Borstal Boy" author
2 As a whole
3 Paramount Pictures founder __ Zukor
4 Fighter at Chancellorsville
5 Fire truck item
6 Characterized by leitmotifs, e.g.
7 So
8 Signs of healing
9 Not just again
10 Dawdle
11 Asthmatics' needs
12 Like sandals
15 Sketch comedy show on Fox
20 Cast supporter?
22 Starter's need
24 __ patriae
25 Renounce
28 Company part
31 Hardly extraneous
33 Imaginary
34 Demilitarized place
35 Solar or lunar phenomenon
36 Astronaut Bean
37 Excite
38 Rounded bolt covers
41 Subject of testimony in a murder trial
42 Nonscoring baccarat card
43 Voltaire's metier
45 Barely maintain
46 Hunger
48 Sitting duck?
50 Completely reliable
52 Actress Ione
56 Book of Samuel character
57 Chapped

by Patrick D. Berry   Thursday, May 18, 2000

SHORTZ SAYS:
The date of this puzzle is a hint to its theme . . . as well as its clues. Note that every clue begins with the same letter of the alphabet. D-lightful!

ACROSS

1 "Do __ others . . ."
5 Disorganized
11 Dirty campaign stuff
14 Drudge of feudal times
15 District in the Philippines
16 Document or diet ending
17 Ducker of military service
19 DiMaggio stat
20 Dewey, e.g.: Abbr.
21 Debonair "bunny man"
22 "Desperately Seeking Susan" actor Quinn
24 "Date film" classic of 1987
28 Devils
31 "Diana," for one
32 Determinant of utility charges
33 Decreases
37 Disclaimer on a sale tag
38 Dobie Gray's "__ Crowd"
40 Deere product: Abbr.
41 Definite agreement
43 Denizen of an aquarium
44 Divorce lawyer on "L.A. Law"
45 Disagreeable air
46 Dauntless ones
50 Dawn
51 Dander
52 Danube locale: Abbr.
55 Decimal point
56 Difficult jump-rope game
61 Defeater of A.E.S.
62 Detach, as a rind
63 Disney lion
64 "Definitely!"
65 Danish, e.g.
66 Decisive time (or theme of this puzzle)

DOWN

1 Dairy or ranch regulator: Abbr.
2 Doofus-y sort
3 Downhill/uphill conveyance
4 Dash __ (write quickly)
5 Drivers' fares
6 Drifting above
7 Doze
8 Delve (into)
9 "Down with the bull!"
10 Droll actor in "Ghostbusters"
11 Day after lundi
12 Densely settled
13 Declining, as embers
18 Dated term for "yours"
23 Drinks popular in hot weather
24 Docked animal parts, maybe
25 Did alpine calls
26 Diocletian's 552
27 Djibouti's Gulf of __
28 Doublet
29 Defunct oil name
30 Duct
34 Dinner scraps
35 Devoted, as friends
36 Duke belongs to it: Abbr.
38 Dollywood locale: Abbr.
39 Department of State chief under Reagan
42 Desiccated
43 Drowsy
45 Describing no more than
46 Daughter's cry?
47 Diminish by degrees
48 Devotional ceremonies
49 Dock sight in Galveston
52 Diminutive amount
53 Daily Bruin sch.
54 Dobbin pulls one
57 Dismiss __ technicality
58 Delivery co.
59 Dice game action
60 Düsseldorf connector

by Alan Arbesfeld

Tuesday, June 6, 2000

SHORTZ SAYS:

This is the only Times crossword that has ever been published without the clue headings Across and Down. Instead, all the clues appear in a single list from 1 to 70. Answers that share a number also share a clue, in a manner for you to discover.

CLUES

1 Fast place
2 It's sent by wire: Abbr.
3 Family dog
4 Will
5 It may bring a box to your house
6 Burn relief
7 Uncle __
8 British facility
9 Catches sight of
10 Arboreal creature with sticky feet
11 Hindu queen
12 Scratched (out)
13 Start of North Carolina's motto
14 "That is __!" (debate charge)
15 Dairy aisle items
16 Thousand __
17 TV newsman Potter and others
18 Piper Cubs, e.g.
19 Couch potato
20 Groups adapted to their environments
21 Singer Sumac
22 Nal, e.g.
23 Doc bloc
24 Members of the family Hydrophidae
25 1946 Literature Nobelist
26 Gen. Rommel
27 Omanl money
28 "Hold on, I've changed my mind!"
29 Retd. check notation
30 Children's game
31 Bring out
32 Knight's list
33 Western New York county
34 Kind of class
35 Salt
36 Classical poem

37 Colonnade around a courtyard
38 Graceful swimmers
39 Gambler's chimera
40 General Tso's chicken maker
41 Variety show
42 Like a delta
43 Second son
44 Texas city, site of the San Jacinto Monument
45 Invoice stamp
46 Superior to a chief warrant officer: Abbr.
47 "__ said . . ."
48 Highway access

49 "Gulliver's Travels" and others
50 Universal ideal
51 Detonation maker
52 Ballet step
53 Hunted items
54 Kind of lily
55 Compos mentis
56 Rug rat
57 It may be the basis of wishful thinking
58 Some roasters
59 Analyst's reply
60 Actor __ Patrick Harris
61 Mardi __
62 Brain
63 Genteel event

64 W.W. I battle site
65 Crud
66 Destined (for)
67 Fictional princess
68 "Peter Pan" man
69 Analyze
70 Wrigglers

by John Duschatko

Wednesday, June 7, 2000

50

SHORTZ SAYS:

This wide-open construction features four 15-letter theme answers, one of which (8-Down) crosses the other three. Not easy to do! A bonus touch that I like is the lively nontheme answer at 20-Across, which is a phrase everyone knows but that has probably never appeared in a crossword before.

ACROSS

1 Nears, with "on"
9 Animal shelter
13 Paper-folding creation
14 Like a rainbow
16 Huey
19 Dancing Astaire
20 "Now I remember!"
21 Fertility clinic stock
22 "__ do"
23 Enjoy a rose
24 Skelton's Kadiddlehopper
25 Scale tone
26 Tucks away
27 Tippler
28 Frau's abode
29 Land of Robert Burns
30 Dewey
35 Humorous illustrator __ Searle
36 Not be calm
37 Oscar-nominated role of 1966
38 King's word
39 Econ. figure
42 Latch (onto)
43 It may be waxed
44 Memories of a whirlwind trip, maybe
45 38-Down's home: Abbr.
46 Pipe cleaner
47 Like sod
48 Louie
51 Full of chutzpah
52 Stets
53 Roasting platform
54 1968 pitcher with six consecutive shutouts

DOWN

1 Orient Express terminus, once
2 Misled
3 "Big Brother is watching you" writer
4 Ecodisaster
5 Besides
6 Pedro or Paulo
7 Well-known, but not well-liked
8 Huey, Dewey and Louie
9 Mike holder
10 Makeshift cradle
11 Hosp. ward
12 Unwavering
15 Gets down to work
17 Brother Castor and sister Olive
18 Attacked
23 Mike holder
24 Kind of skin
26 Rock that may hold fossils
27 Longtime "Today" show personality
29 Contractor's info
30 Like "Othello"
31 Continues, after a fashion
32 Nebulous
33 Critically injure
34 Jean Valjean, at the start of "Les Misérables"
38 Overseas carrier
39 Tongue, anatomically
40 Cooking agent
41 "The Scarlet Letter" woman
43 Doesn't wear well
44 __ stiff
46 7th-century date
47 Relig. leaders
49 Tax form info: Abbr.
50 Kind of care

by Mark Diehl   Thursday, August 10, 2000

SHORTZ SAYS:

This 68-word grid contains ten 15-letter answers spanning the grid, with 8-Down intersecting the nine going across. As typical with Bob Klahn, he spices up the puzzle with lively vocabulary, and the grid doesn't have a single unnecessary black square.

ACROSS

1 Comprehensive insurance plans
16 Cause for celebration
17 Summer runners
18 Romeo's last words
19 1995 role for Kenneth Branagh
20 Empty talk
21 Start of a religious observance?
22 Command level: Abbr.
24 Personal involvement
28 Provider of a pick-me-up?
30 What 1 might mean: Abbr.
33 Contract provision
37 "Leaving Home" author
38 "Guys and Dolls" song
39 Purged
40 March figures, for short
41 They're made to measure
42 Mtge. units
43 Broken
46 Trouble spots?
49 Capital of Moravia
50 It takes a beating
54 Team for which George Plimpton once played
58 "Ain't Misbehavin' " tune
59 Like 101, to 102?

DOWN

1 Sons of, in Hebrew
2 Wagered
3 "Tales of a Wayside Inn" bell town
4 Swell
5 Hootchy-___
6 "The Untouchables" composer Morricone
7 Shouts of triumph
8 Promise to marry
9 "___ be in England . . ."
10 Rule, in Rouen
11 1969 Peace Prize grp.
12 Sure thing
13 Noodle concoction
14 Clear
15 Network: Abbr.
21 Dependent
22 Shine
23 Paramecium, e.g.
24 Popeye's creator
25 Letter before qoph
26 Like a farm
27 Baron Münchhausen
29 Places of refuge
30 Something to sip
31 Together
32 "Phooey!"
34 Nike competitor
35 Flap
36 "Summer and Smoke" heroine
42 L.A.'s San ___ Bay
44 Pernod flavoring
45 Big name in juices
46 "Comin ___!" (1981 3-D western)
47 Ice cream flavor, briefly
48 Prefix with -itis
49 Novelist ___ Easton Ellis
50 Classic dress
51 Courtroom cover-up
52 Combined, in Compiègne
53 One of a group of 40-Across
55 Letters starting many military plane names
56 French pronoun
57 Drawing

by Bob Klahn

Friday, September 29, 2000

SHORTZ SAYS:
This puzzle's clever theme is signaled by the circled letters in the middle of the grid. For the constructor to get all these multi-checked letters to work could not have been easy.

ACROSS

1 Passport feature
6 Role for Ingrid
10 Bridge toll unit
14 Overthrowing a base, e.g.
15 Select
16 Prehistoric terror, informally
17 Superhero's home
19 Go on and on
20 "Look, up in the __!"
21 Playboy centerfold
22 Authority
23 32 pieces and a board
25 Speed: Abbr.
26 Certain teas
29 They go well with plaids
31 Diamond unit
32 Asian plains
35 River to Hades
36 Stayed at home
37 Best Picture of 1958
40 Dress store section
42 Feeling puffed up
43 Players in a dome, once
45 Taken care of
46 "__ Te Ching"
47 More skittish
51 Like much notebook paper
53 "The Unity of India" writer
54 Symbol on a cape
57 Et __
58 Superhero's nickname
60 Drunks
61 Smooth (out)
62 Baseball Hall-of-Famer Combs
63 Deuce taker
64 "Pretty Woman" co-star
65 Berate

DOWN

1 Grad sch. classes
2 Trudge
3 Pretentious
4 Commercial suffix with "Sav-"
5 Prognosticator
6 Computer programs have them
7 Whoppers
8 Mooring spots
9 Gore and Bundy
10 Gillette brand
11 Superhero's skill
12 Filmed, in Hollywood slang
13 Praises lavishly
18 Slapstick comedy items
22 Clog (up)
23 Encourager
24 "SportsZone" airer
26 IBM products
27 Partake of
28 Superhero's undoing
30 Fictional Simon
32 Used a bench
33 Mao __-tung
34 Wasser in the winter
36 Smart-alecky
38 Belt tightener?
39 Altar reply
41 Snitched
42 Scans
43 Finally
44 Expert on spars and stars
45 Catch a wave
48 Catch
49 Mister, in Mendoza
50 Radiated
52 "__ does it"
54 Architect Saarinen
55 Talk up
56 Huskies' load
58 Russian plane
59 Middle of XXX

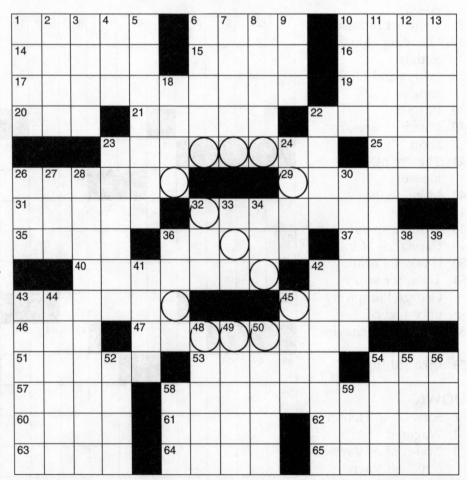

by Bill Zais

Tuesday, October 31, 2000

SHORTZ SAYS:
Saturday Times crosswords don't often have themes, but this one is an exception. It features four interlocking theme answers and a hint to the trick at 41-Down.

53

ACROSS

1 Big moneymaker
8 Chairs may hold them
14 Still, in a way
15 "Some nerve!"
16 Firmly formed
17 Jam and cram again
18 __ Francis of hockey fame
19 Dweller in Clydebank
21 Paris Opera part
22 Unlock
24 In print
25 Teaching venues
26 __ Brainard, the Absent-Minded Professor
27 Smashing
30 Use a shuttle
31 Kind of hole
33 Plenty
35 Trying cases, plea bargaining, etc.?
39 Jackson of jazz
40 Prefix meaning "likeness"
41 Pocket
42 Expected to happen
45 Pinkerton, e.g.
48 Morsels
50 "Well, lookee here!"
51 Art school name
54 Artifice
55 Hit or miss
57 "__ else fails . . ."
58 Brewer's product
60 Words before a fight?
62 When repeated, not much in the way of news
63 One who puts on a cap
64 Pizazz
65 Some disbelievers

DOWN

1 Sounded like a rook
2 Cave dwellers
3 Unite
4 Pickup artist's line?
5 Checked out
6 Suffix with 55-Across
7 Volstead Act opponents
8 Tough area
9 50's political monogram
10 Like some organs
11 Don of England, e.g.
12 Musée d'Orsay locale
13 Most dependable
15 They chase flies
20 One who works for the Police Gazette?
23 Town connected by bridge to Windsor
28 __ sense
29 Director's opposite
32 Bad marks in high school, maybe
34 Dentists' convention?
35 Like some plans
36 1962 musical choreographed by Bob Fosse
37 It's nonreturnable
38 Mixer
41 Without any chance at all (and a phonetic hint to this puzzle's theme)
43 Enticing
44 Up, in a way
46 Ballet position
47 Arp contemporary
49 Where questions are asked
52 Fraternity letter
53 Giants and Pirates, e.g.
56 Sound units
59 Dress (up)
61 It may be picked

by David J. Kahn

Saturday, December 2, 2000

ACROSS

1 Building supports
6 "I see," facetiously
10 Not latched
14 Zero Mostel role of 1964
15 Color of some wine grapes
16 Cracked
17 Insomniac's need
19 Crack, in a way
20 Otologist's study
21 Company founded by Steve Case
22 Newspaper read at Notre Dame
24 Oliver's wife on "Green Acres"
26 Common Market: Abbr.
28 Lower
29 Vietnam was part of it
32 Actress Thurman
34 Travel widely
35 Raises
36 Arctic native
37 Fallacious reasoner
40 The Who's "Tommy" and others
41 China aster, e.g.
42 Scot's wear
43 Taken in
44 Naples's home: Abbr.
45 Carte start
46 Soapmaking substance
51 Modern data holder
53 Moreover
54 1970 Kinks hit
55 Sorrowful cry
57 Rebuffs
59 Roulette bet
60 Troubles
61 Hubert Humphrey's running mate, 1968
64 1982 title role for Meryl Streep

65 Nettle
66 Judge, at times
67 Geologists' divisions
68 Proof word
69 Dental stuff

DOWN

1 What "ipso" means
2 Fancy part of Los Angeles
3 Loath
4 Some whiskey
5 Print tint
6 Caught some rays, perhaps
7 Kachina doll maker
8 Framework piece
9 Capital of Loiret

10 Major can maker
11 Chief of staff under George Bush
12 Dean's concern
13 Skip it
18 Very much
23 Exec's degree
25 Apprehensive feeling
27 Overthrow
30 Big name in the ad biz
31 Poker supplies
33 N.L. East team
36 Counting everything
37 Cousin of reggae
38 Art shop buy
39 Eagles' home
40 Delay

41 Prince Valiant's wife
43 Sewing machine attachments
44 Kind of insurance
46 Writer Marilyn — Savant
47 Car hood, in Britain
48 Consult
49 Enduring hits
50 Duck hunter's boots
52 Angry reactions
55 Sage
56 Rearrange, say
58 Kids' TV character
62 Uncooperative one
63 Noted 62-Down

by Peter Gordon

Thursday, December 14, 2000

SHORTZ SAYS:
The constructor of this crossword (a Times regular) carries each of his theme ideas as far as possible, adding multiple layers, if appropriate—and does so with skill and flair. Here is an excellent example.

ACROSS

1 Was in the running for
8 Summer dress feature
14 They often start "Here"
16 Jim Palmer, once
17 Where The Gazette is published
18 Kind of club
19 Hoops stat.
20 Forfeit again
22 Benjamin Disraeli, e.g.
23 African pullover
24 Schoolmarmish
26 Mr. __ of "Peter Pan"
28 "There it is!"
30 August birthstone
34 Siesta time
36 In direct competition
38 CD-__
39 Inventor who inspired this puzzle
41 Get spliced
42 Parts left out
45 Fosters, for one
48 First name in mystery writing
49 Sri Lanka export
51 Ninny
52 "__ Stars," #1 hit for Freddy Martin, 1934
54 Symbol of punctuality
56 Ale relative
59 Waterside accommodations provider
61 Duffel
64 Rare birth
66 Weigh heavily
68 Sewer, maybe
69 Screenwriter's start
70 Auto gauge shower
71 Speech enliveners

DOWN

1 Rope material
2 Per
3 Like Errol Flynn
4 Old Polo Grounds favorite
5 Hung back
6 Take __ (look)
7 Muse of comedy
8 Draw game?
9 Valuable deposit
10 QB protectors
11 Hawaiian storm
12 16-Across, for short
13 "I'm all ears"
15 Pavement caution
21 Goes over
23 Dancer's partner?
25 Wall St. event
26 Vodka brand, informally
27 First lady with bangs
29 Chestnut, e.g.
31 Spur part
32 Like krypton
33 Lavished love (on)
35 Comic Philips
37 Elusive one
38 Timber tree with colored inner bark
40 When some footballs are hiked
43 Like many doors
44 French pronoun
46 Good name for a girl writing a postscript?
47 Beckett title name
50 Athens's state, in ancient times
53 Call off
55 Euripides play
56 Commuter's run?
57 Pride of Israel
58 Dugout shelter
60 When half of rush hours occur: Abbr.
61 "Viva Maria!" actress, 1965
62 Play to __
63 Some G.M. cars
65 Book after Ezra: Abbr.
67 Part of X-X-X

by David J. Kahn

Friday, December 29, 2000

56

SHORTZ SAYS:
As mentioned on the puzzle of July 24, 1998, the record for the lowest number of black squares in a standard 15×15-square grid was 21. This puzzle set a new record with just 20. Still, the vocabulary in it sparkles, and it doesn't have a single bad entry.

ACROSS

1 Monarchy or parliamentary democracy
16 A little too clever
17 Oven item
18 Stray
19 Join securely
20 1984 skiing gold medalist
21 Many cottage dwellers
23 Diner orders
25 Arab League V.I.P.'s
26 Putdowns
27 Connecting points
28 Sacks
29 Piece of neckwear
32 "Let's Get __" (1973 #1 hit)
33 Star, maybe
34 '93 Sugar Bowl champs
35 W.W. I troops: Abbr.
36 Ace of clubs?
37 Aristophanes comedy, with "The"
38 New Orleans sandwich, informally
39 Solid swats
40 Emitted steam
43 Promotes
44 Kind of warfare
45 Half of the "Wayne's World" duo
47 Author LeShan
48 Wall Street gambit
51 Camper's need
52 Comments from co-workers

DOWN

1 Former German duchy known for a breed of dog
2 Really ham it up, redundantly
3 Found out about
4 N.Y.C. subway
5 Snickers
6 "__, she's mine . . ." (Manfred Mann lyric)
7 Columnist Herb and others
8 Farm prefix
9 Study of lakes and ponds
10 __-Cross Championship Racing
11 Complains
12 Baseball stat
13 Church offering
14 Turn out
15 Paris parents
22 It may follow four or six, but not five
24 Silence
26 Like most cemetery plots
28 Sports org. owned by Fox
29 In which 49 is 100
30 Rash
31 What tubas play
33 Naïf
34 Place of interest?
36 Napoleon's birthplace
37 One of the brothers Grimm
38 Bill
39 Potato dishes
40 Screening device
41 Separate
42 Not in
43 Golfers' bane
46 To __ (just so)
49 Mil. titles
50 Encouraging word

by Joe DiPietro   Friday, January 19, 2001

SHORTZ SAYS:
Speaking of record-breaking, this puzzle may well hold the record for the most theme entries of its type in a standard 15×15 grid. I won't reveal exactly what type this is—you'll feel proud when you discover the secret for yourself.

ACROSS

1 "One Man's San Francisco" author
5 __ doble (Latin dance)
9 Some Olympians, nowadays
13 Stare impertinently
14 Slogan
16 Algebra topic
18 Like some rats
19 "You there?"
20 Org. that banned DDT
21 Knock over
24 Critic, at times
25 Pay the entire check
28 Fertilizer sources
31 What a cedilla indicates
33 Talk incessantly
34 Turnstile part
37 It can be found in oil
40 Game in which jacks are highest trumps
41 Inflammatory diseases
42 Radiate
43 Ripens
45 Monterrey jack?
46 Pinch-hitting great Manny __
49 Super __ (old video game standard)
50 Washington, to Lafayette
52 Fed
54 Chafing dish fuel
57 1947 Best Picture nominee
62 Waste away
63 Answer to the riddle "Dressed in summer, naked in winter"
64 1980's Davis Cup captain
65 Hits a fly
66 City on the Gulf of Aqaba

DOWN

1 Serving with vin
2 Río contents
3 Airline with King David Lounges
4 "Nashville" co-star
5 Outdoor dining spot
6 N.C. State plays in it
7 H. Rider Haggard novel
8 Alphabet trio
9 They talk too much
10 Angrily harangue
11 "__ Mio"
12 "Sí" man?
14 Break activity, perhaps
15 "What's that?"
17 Saw with the grain
21 Knocking noises
22 Kind of triangle
23 Louis Botha, notably
25 Recipe abbr.
26 Fleece
27 Black key
29 Guarantee
30 Blender setting
32 The Rhumba King
34 Together, in music
35 Some mail designations: Abbr.
36 San __, Calif.
38 Something in writing?
39 An American in Paris, perhaps
43 Dugong's cousin
44 Half of quattordici
46 A Gabor sister
47 Cruel people
48 Choppers
51 Part of a baby bottle
53 Artist Gerard __ Borch
54 Flies away
55 "Me neither"
56 1977 Scott Turow book
58 Greek letters
59 "Ker-bam!"
60 Quod __ faciendum
61 Subway wish

by Peter Gordon   Thursday, March 8, 2001

58

SHORTZ SAYS:
When you see Cathy Millhauser's byline on a puzzle, you can be virtually certain that your laugh muscles are about to get a workout. Here she takes four common phrases and puts a punny twist on them in a very specific way.

ACROSS

1 Double dates
5 Old newspaper sections
10 Something to nibble on with Beaujolais
14 "Alfred" and "Judith" composer
15 Grown
16 __ Minor
17 Agitate
18 Lofty
19 Pipsqueak
20 "Flood cleanup wears me out!"
23 Line on an invoice
24 "Gotcha!"
25 Bridal path
26 Wilt Chamberlain was one
28 Big name in fine china
30 Strut
31 "Health club exercise is so boring!"
36 Jazzman Allison
39 Franz of operetta fame
40 Tout's concern
41 "Military service leaves me pooped!"
44 Zip-zip
45 Sweethearts
49 Lamb Chop enlivener Lewis
50 Phone menu imperative
54 __ sense
55 One sense, figuratively
56 "Driving takes away all your energy!"
59 As one, at Orly
61 Old-style copier
62 Reformer Jacob
63 Ordered to go
64 Pretty blue
65 Memo starter
66 Irritable
67 Battery components?
68 Kind of money

DOWN

1 Of the ankle
2 Squirm
3 Out, at the library
4 One who gets what's coming
5 Actress Oakes of "CHiPs"
6 Kitchens have them
7 Like some pregnancies
8 Football Hall-of-Famer Matson
9 1930's Goldwyn star Anna
10 It now has a Union: Abbr.
11 Soak
12 Painkiller dosage phrase
13 Sleep on it
21 Long, for short
22 Louver part
27 Certain vocal part
29 Submissive type
30 It borders the state of Amazonas
32 Kind of pot
33 Still
34 Greek antepenultimate
35 Stay behind
36 She kneads people
37 Left alone
38 Campaign dirty tricks
42 Money guarantor, for short
43 Designer Schiaparelli
46 Blur remover
47 Complete
48 Got smart with
50 Cup or purse
51 Twin of myth
52 Put forth, in a way
53 They may be tapped for the stage
57 Third in a Latin recital
58 "Trinity" novelist
60 What a mess!

by Cathy Millhauser

Thursday, March 15, 2001

SHORTZ SAYS:

Almost all of us had or were at least familiar with decoder rings when we were kids, for writing and receiving secret messages. This construction adopts the decoder ring idea for a puzzle within a puzzle—the kind of novel twist in a crossword that I love.

ACROSS

1 Scotland's __ Fyne
5 It's nothing to speak of
10 Perennial presidential campaign issue
14 Memo phrase
15 Part of a U.S. census category
16 "Did you __?!"
17 Bound
18 Manly apparel
19 __ avis
20 Half of a decoder ring
23 Former nuclear power org.
24 "Còmo __ usted?"
25 Maserati, e.g.
29 It gives you an out
34 The Buckeyes: Abbr.
35 Heralded
38 What a rubber produces?
39 Secret message
43 Hall-of-Fame coach Mike
44 Author Wiesel
45 Clay, after transformation
46 English essayist Sir Richard
48 Unpleasant ones
51 Landers and others
54 Opus __
55 Other half of the decoder ring
61 Thailand, once
62 More than hot
63 Gave the go-ahead
65 French 101 verb
66 Pluralizers
67 Woman of the haus
68 Its motto is L'Étoile du Nord: Abbr.
69 Thomas Jefferson, religiously
70 Inevitability

DOWN

1 Not-so-apt word for Abner
2 Suitable for service
3 Shore catch
4 One who's beat but good?
5 "Be well"
6 Catchphrase from "Clueless"
7 Poppycock
8 They may be made with Bibles
9 Present
10 Be rough with the reins
11 Flattened figure
12 Earthwork
13 Madrid Mme.
21 Big holiday mo.
22 Notched
25 Makes origami
26 Comparatively healthy
27 Deluxe accommodations
28 All-night party
30 Early auto
31 Zhou __
32 Move like a 3-Down
33 Tournament round
36 Nothing
37 Smile
40 Classic Jaguar
41 Hit 1980's–90's NBC drama
42 Car safety feature
47 Coveted
49 Et __ (footnote abbr.)
50 Warn
52 Hospital figure
53 Former East German secret police
55 Tubes in the kitchen
56 Tale
57 Marvel Comics heroes
58 Jeanne d'Arc et al.: Abbr.
59 Gumbo component
60 Without ice
61 Relig. training ground
64 Company in Italy?

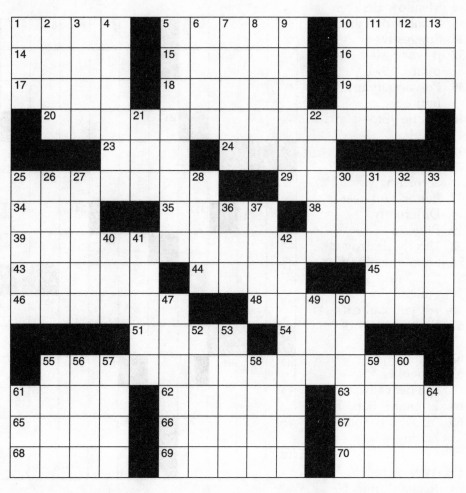

by William I. Johnston

Thursday, March 29, 2001

60

SHORTZ SAYS:
Mel Taub has been a Times constructor since the 1950's. He's best known for his Puns and Anagrams puzzles, which appear several times a year on the Sunday puzzle page. Here is a more traditional crossword for which he directed the construction in an adult education course on crosswords at a Manhattan YMCA. Before the course began, he proposed the theme, which I preapproved. Then he and his students, in class, jointly produced the grid and the clues.

ACROSS

1 "__," said Tom presently
5 Not chronic
10 Limey's quaff
14 N.Y.S.E. competitor
15 General denial?
16 Big partygoer?
17 "__," said Tom unremittingly
20 Hood's gun
21 Pond cover
22 Gladiator's place
23 On the main
24 Word before juris or generis
25 "__," said Tom fittingly
33 Snappish
34 Meadow denizen
35 Symbol of solidity
36 Suggestive
37 It was tested on Bikini, 1954
39 Polynesian amulet figure
40 "Little" Stowe girl
41 "Fudge!"
42 Baffler
43 "__," said Tom accordingly
47 Bettor's interest
48 Differently
49 Pretend
52 Utterly destroyed
54 State touching Can.
57 "__," said Tom patiently
60 All you can eat
61 Early settlers of Iceland
62 Top
63 Provokes splenetically
64 Emulates Babe Ruth
65 "__," said Tom haltingly

DOWN

1 Reagan cabinet member
2 Mme. Bovary
3 Let
4 Outside: Prefix
5 "Crouching Tiger, Hidden Dragon" director
6 Jackie who starred in "Tom Sawyer," 1930
7 Voice of America org.
8 It has a point
9 Work unit
10 "All in the Family" role
11 Ready for plucking
12 Saudi Arabia neighbor
13 Maja painter
18 Nice to nosh
19 Gray-brown
23 Aesthetically pretentious
24 Macedonian's neighbor
25 Spread around
26 Cry to anchor men
27 "Platoon" prize
28 Sandal strap
29 Many a skit actor
30 Complaints
31 Bilked
32 Evade
37 Dangle
38 Lifting device
39 Webster's Unabridged, e.g.
41 Sawyer of ABC
42 Linguine sauce
44 "Communist Manifesto" co-author
45 Feed
46 Gets around
49 Poodle name
50 Mideast ruler
51 Man, but not Woman
52 Be sure
53 Uttar Pradesh tourist site
54 Hankering
55 Spanish building topper
56 Quarter
58 Politicos with jobs
59 Raven's call

by Mel Taub and crossword class   Wednesday, April 25, 2001

SHORTZ SAYS:

Before he was even out of high school, Trip Payne knew that he wanted to be a professional crossword constructor and editor. Here is a fine example of his work, featuring a funny quotation and stacking of theme entries. Incidentally, Trip is the youngest person (at 24) ever to win the American Crossword Puzzle Tournament. He also won $32,000 on "Who Wants to Be a Millionaire."

ACROSS

1 Overthrown leader
5 Not out
10 See 61-Down
14 Actress Lamarr
15 Beau's gift
16 Till fill
17 Speaker of the quip starting at 20-Across
19 It has the spirit
20 Start of a quip
22 Slightest
23 Word of agreement
24 Sharp flavor
26 "Kate & Allie" actress Meyers
27 Young fowl
31 It could be stuffed
33 Old station identification
35 Had
36 Main city of Devon
37 Quip, part 2
40 Haunt
43 Jeff Lynne group
44 "My Uncle" star
48 Chekhov uncle
49 It should set off alarms
51 Informal footwear
52 Flutter
53 One of the Volcano Islands, for short
55 Jobs site
57 Quip, part 3
62 Subjoins
63 End of the quip
64 Saddle, e.g.
65 Tel Aviv-born person
66 French jeweler Lalique
67 "Chickery Chick" bandleader
68 Smithery employee
69 Genesis source

DOWN

1 "The Glamorous Life" singer
2 Sewing machine attachments
3 Shelley's elegy to Keats
4 Some needles
5 __ cantabile (gentle, sad song)
6 Whistle maker?
7 China setting
8 Persisted in
9 Paper
10 Spots
11 Ticked off
12 Merry
13 "You naughty person!"
18 Start of many addresses
21 Paul V's papal predecessor
25 Part of w.p.m.
28 They can be rolled
29 Tribal language
30 Bank
32 It's just not right
34 Follow
36 TV spinoff of 1980
38 Carrier name until 1997
39 Biblical judge
40 Plant gametes
41 "I wouldn't do that"
42 Winter break, of a sort
45 Person with a loss
46 Sexton's duty
47 Summer drink
49 Platform on the back of an elephant
50 Kind of shell
54 Houdini's birth name
56 Really rains
58 Princely family name of old
59 Transient
60 Bern is on it
61 With 10-Across, skier's aid
62 "Shoot!"

by Trip Payne

Thursday, May 3, 2001

62

SHORTZ SAYS:
The secret of this puzzle's theme is revealed at 62- and 16-Across. The theme itself appears in the six longest Across answers. That's a lot of theme material, with a crackerjack construction besides.

ACROSS

1 Quirky 70's–80's band
5 "Evita" role
8 Give confidence to
14 Mountain stat.
15 Agreement abroad
16 See 62-Across
17 Previous
19 Attacked violently
20 Bejeweled adornment
21 Bush Sr. headed it
23 "Ici on __ français"
24 Like a street urchin
27 Jungle queen of 50's TV
30 Retaliation, in part?
31 They're affected by the ionosphere
34 Totenberg of NPR
38 True up
39 Island off India's coast
40 Theaters
41 Father of Enos
42 Spread out, timewise
44 Cup at a grease joint
45 James of "Marcus Welby, M.D."
46 Movie house popcorn choice
52 Tryon novel, with "The"
53 You might need a paddle to do this
54 Brilliance
58 Stingers?
60 Went around in circles?
62 With 16-Across, the theme of this puzzle
63 Too late for the E.R.
64 Oddball
65 Big name in swimwear
66 Pay stub abbr.
67 Frank or Francis

DOWN

1 Skilled
2 "The Time Machine" people
3 Designer Wang
4 Oppress
5 Bill's partner
6 Funny feeling
7 Children's song refrain
8 Halifax clock setting: Abbr.
9 Pull into
10 Fergie, formally
11 In __ (unborn)
12 Empire
13 Cosmetician Lauder
18 Begin to catch up with
22 Filmmaker with total creative control
25 Spotted, to Tweety
26 "Angela's Ashes" follow-up
27 Sp. ladies
28 In good health
29 Get to work on Time?
32 Modifying word
33 Go for the gold
34 1939 Garbo role
35 Worldwide: Abbr.
36 Beverage brand
37 Org.
40 Eye bank donation
42 Scoreboard line under RHE, maybe
43 George W. deg.
44 Sun-dried, as beef
46 Ness et al.
47 Ready, as a sail
48 __ Island red
49 Hollow rock
50 Lightheaded
51 No-brainer?
55 Nutcase
56 The King's middle name
57 Profits
59 __-Cone
61 Pops

by Alan Arbesfeld   **Wednesday, May 23, 2001**

SHORTZ SAYS:

Most crossword constructors would have been satisfied with the three theme entries at 17-, 36- and 57-Across. Will Johnston added a fourth theme entry at 7-Down, turning a merely good puzzle into a great one.

ACROSS

1 Emphatic agreement
5 Pitcher Shawn __
10 See 48-Down
14 Circular announcement
15 Ring
16 Mine, in Montréal
17 X
20 Unusual
21 Pulls down, so to speak
22 Méditerranée, par exemple
23 You may flirt with it
26 Thun's river
27 "Farewell, My Lovely" novelist
31 Neighbor of an Afghani
34 Bohr's study
35 __ y plata (Montana's motto)
36 X
40 Hollywood job: Abbr.
41 It means nothing to Nicolette
42 "Shake, Rattle and Roll" singer
43 Sticky situation
46 Crop
47 Sorry soul
49 Authority on diamonds?
52 "I don't buy it"
55 7,926 miles, for the earth
57 X
60 __-eyed
61 Judging group
62 Fall preceder, perhaps
63 Throw out
64 Like God, in a fire-and-brimstone sermon
65 Some queens

DOWN

1 Land bordering Bhutan
2 Equivocal answer
3 Dramatist Rice
4 North Platte locale: Abbr.
5 No dessert for a dieter
6 Climbs, in a way
7 X X X
8 Source of lean red meat
9 Clinton, e.g.: Abbr.
10 Baseless rumor
11 Archer of myth
12 Square setting
13 Faults
18 Make a father
19 Neato
24 Less woolly, perhaps
25 Author Janowitz
26 Singer DiFranco
28 Hang out
29 Noted Folies Bergère designer
30 Like some outlooks
31 Operation Desert Storm target
32 Lipton, Inc. brand
33 Girl lead-in
34 Conflagrant
37 What cleats increase
38 Greg's sitcom wife
39 Labor org. since 1935
44 They may be sour
45 Whimper
46 How brutes behave
48 With 10-Across, ocelot and margay
49 Complete change of mind
50 Excellence
51 Gets ready
52 "Over here!"
53 Minuteman's place
54 They have participating M.D.'s
56 James of jazz
58 Grp. monitoring emissions
59 __ Clemente

by William I. Johnston

Thursday, May 24, 2001

64

SHORTZ SAYS:
If you'd like to delay learning the secret of this puzzle as long as possible—the special nature of the entire construction—don't look at the last clue (65-Down) until the end. It explains the puzzle's amazing theme.

ACROSS

1 Besides
5 "Cómo __ usted?"
9 City near Düsseldorf
14 They hang around
16 Accustom: Var.
17 Southern lights
19 Take the conn
20 Noted monologuist
21 Hwys.
22 W. Hemisphere grp.
24 Scope
26 Window bases
29 "Mon Oncle" star Jacques
31 It comes before a dropped name
34 29 for copper, e.g.: Abbr.
35 Choo-choo's sound
37 Lowest in importance
39 Game you can lose only once
42 Fastening devices
43 Labor
44 Roger of "Cheers"
45 Cardinal's insignia
46 Those, to José
48 Choker
50 Out of port
52 Scull propeller
53 Der __ (Konrad Adenauer)
55 Musical Horne
58 Having no chips left to bet
63 Explosive stuff
66 Sleeping perch
67 Most minuscule
68 Queen __ lace
69 "What __?"
70 J.F.K. arrivals

DOWN

1 "What a pity!"
2 Boor
3 Dam's counterpart
4 Oklahoma Indian
5 Detergent brand
6 What some pups grow up to be
7 50/50 test choice
8 Org.
9 Poetic adverb
10 Marching band drum
11 Brunei and Oman, e.g.
12 Toledo's lake
13 1987 role for Costner
15 Actor Flynn
18 Perfectly
23 Wirehair of film
25 Small brook
26 Daring feat
27 Attic covering, maybe
28 Found's partner
29 Pamplona runners
30 Yours: Fr.
32 Cosmetician Lauder
33 Hot seasons in Québec
34 They might be fine
36 Aware of
38 Architect Saarinen
40 "Gotcha"
41 It parallels the radius
47 Brining need
49 Tough tests
51 Feel
52 Hall's singing partner
53 Razor brand
54 "Dianetics" author __ Hubbard
56 One-named artist
57 Winter air
59 Pitcher Tiant
60 Directors Ang and Spike
61 M.I.T. part: Abbr.
62 Captures
64 "__ a girl!"
65 Point value in Scrabble of every letter in this puzzle

by Peter Gordon   Tuesday, June 5, 2001

SHORTZ SAYS:
Besides being funny, this puzzle is also elegant: The four main theme entries appear in two intersecting pairs. Just think of all the theme possibilities that Cathy Millhauser must have rejected until she found ones to cross on the necessary letters!

ACROSS

1 Greek's sixth
5 "King Cotton" composer
10 Wax
14 Knee-slapper
15 Void
16 Road condition?
17 After 34-Down, an order to a witch?
19 Leeds's river
20 Leads (in)
21 Stomped
23 Mozart article
24 Psalms interjection
25 On the main deck
28 It may be under your tongue
32 Dropped a line
33 Violent struggle
36 Med. care group
37 Tennessee's state flower
38 Shoe sole material
39 Number after cinco
40 Palindromic diarist
41 Game with a 40-card deck
42 Rally creators
43 Call for
45 Like fan-tan and tangrams
47 Feather in Juan's cap?
50 Italy's Isola d'___
51 They're polar
54 Residences
57 Brandenburg trio
58 After 34-Down, an order to a chiropractor?
60 Chutzpah
61 Husband of Bathsheba
62 Fast sport
63 Some are electric
64 Trimming targets
65 Load

DOWN

1 Mao contemporary
2 Almost forever
3 After 34-Down, an order to an arrowsmith?
4 Ones who might say, "God, no!"?
5 Mouthed off
6 Neighbor of Man.
7 Modulars, e.g.
8 Bolivian capital
9 High-pH
10 Plots, in a way
11 Fulminate
12 Fiend
13 Cig
18 Golf champ Els
22 Oodles
25 Strong string
26 Hatch from Utah
27 Make
29 After 34-Down, an order to an E.P.A. administrator
30 Pianist Gilels et al.
31 It's catching
34 See 17- and 58-Across and 3- and 29-Down
35 Kind of minister
38 October honoree
39 Annual El Paso events
41 Miss's equal
42 "The Hobbit" hero Baggins
44 Periods of rain, often
46 Moors
48 Half a comedy duo
49 Computer acronym
51 Sidle
52 Picture of health?
53 Prefix with com
55 Hence
56 Misrepresent
59 ___ Kan

by Cathy Millhauser   **Thursday, August 30, 2001**

66

SHORTZ SAYS:
Brendan Emmett Quigley, a guitarist for the Boston-based rock band Hip Tanaka, brings a certain hipness to the Times crossword, a feature that is not usually known for being hip. My favorite part of this puzzle is 23-Across, a colorful, funny phrase that everyone has heard, but which I'm sure no one had ever thought to put in a crossword before.

ACROSS

1 N.H.L. division: Abbr.
4 Is wearing
9 With 11-Down, "Casablanca" site
14 Word with caddy or bag
15 Prefix with arthritis
16 Online sales
17 __ sgt. (police rank)
18 "Never!"
20 They undergo bonding
22 Glossy finish
23 Angry parent's yell
27 Patricia of "Breakfast at Tiffany's"
28 Order members
29 Political cartoonist Rall
32 Pindar, for one
34 Enlarged river, perhaps
37 Connie Francis's 1960 film debut
41 Have no more good ideas
42 Sticks
43 "Undoubtedly"
44 Resentments
45 Discharge
49 Comment about a sad but memorable exit
53 Numbskulls
55 Michael who starred in TV's "It's a Great Life"
56 1975 Four Seasons hit
60 Legal rep.
61 Exuded
62 "Today" co-host
63 Strive (for)
64 Newspaper opinion pieces
65 Drops out of the bidding
66 Summer in Sèvres

DOWN

1 When many duels take place
2 Raise canines?
3 One of the Jacksons
4 "Want to explain that?"
5 Silvery gray
6 Sault __ Marie
7 Wine: Prefix
8 Hotel lobby sign
9 Splendid
10 Words to elicit recognition
11 See 9-Across
12 Waste, as time
13 Insidious
19 Some acct. money
21 Royal address?
24 Kwanzaa principle
25 Heavy drinker
26 Acura model
29 American acquisition of 2001
30 Musician's gift
31 Purchase for a disguise
33 "__ Rosenkavalier"
34 "El Capitán" composer
35 Looker
36 They may be fixed
37 Lopsided, as a grin
38 Color
39 Dash widths
40 Mishandled
44 A thing unto __
46 Native Arizonan
47 "That makes sense!"
48 Exactly
49 Enticed
50 Engine covers
51 Off-road goer, briefly
52 Traditional letter closer
53 Breakfast place, for short
54 Drift (off)
56 Try to win over
57 __ Tiago
58 Actor Brynner
59 Multivolume ref.

by Brendan Emmett Quigley   Wednesday, November 7, 2001

A small spoiler here: While this puzzle looks like it's themeless (it contains only 68 answers after all), it does, in fact, have a five-part theme. The constructor is a member of the math department at Santa Clara University.

ACROSS

1 Shrimp
8 "Jeopardy!" contestants, e.g.
14 Transports over a slick surface
15 One of Gabe's "sweathogs," in 70's TV
16 Aggressive plugging
17 News time, maybe
18 It's opposite Juárez
19 Great facility
20 Parodied
21 A community may have one
24 Sheltered
25 Reason for a badge
27 Part of some e-mail addresses
28 Like some locks
29 High class?: Abbr.
30 Make a big splash, maybe
33 Hard butter?
34 Where Indian movies are produced
35 God's first word?
38 "It's __!"
40 Dynasty after Ch'in
41 Lyric poem
43 Place to use a lorgnette
44 Code name
46 __ for the money
47 Decks out
49 Film statistic
51 Protected wildlife
52 Tough
54 Bloody Mary alternative
55 Oil sites
56 Movie preview, essentially
57 Makes even smoother

DOWN

1 Sellout profiteer
2 Support group

3 Half a Beatles title
4 Rob __ (Scotch manhattans)
5 Truckee River source
6 Skating silver medalist at Albertville
7 What that is in Toledo
8 Claims
9 It's raised on a farm
10 Was no dummy
11 Wrap
12 Chocolate candy brand
13 Saw, e.g.
14 Support group?
19 Squares and such

22 Cries while hunting
23 Fight to keep the faith
26 Certain investment, briefly
28 It may make the cut
31 3.75 feet, once
32 Rock music's __ Fighters
33 Reach by drilling
34 Great thing to hit
35 Kind of truck
36 Revisionists?
37 Moon of Saturn
38 Some buzzers
39 Like Shelley's "Frankenstein"

42 Chinese transliteration system
44 Some western scenery
45 They, in Tours
48 Picked up
50 Poet __ Wheeler Wilcox
52 Where to see a round of shots
53 Wildcat's opponent in the 1998 Final Four

by Byron L. Walden

Friday, November 23, 2001

SHORTZ SAYS:
Imagine a crossword with three unchecked squares (see 36-Across), which, nevertheless, every solver can fill in with complete certainty. Patrick Merrell, a cartoonist and humorist by profession, created this novelty, which was one of The Times's most talked-about puzzles of the year.

ACROSS

1 __ Hall
6 Trudge
10 Site of many walls
14 2002 Olympics venue
15 "__ mouse!"
16 "Exodus" author
17 Brickworker
18 "Zounds!"
19 Money maker
20 Suffix with origin
21 Do this if 36-Across is two letters
23 These go in 36-Across
25 Rate __ (be perfect)
26 B.O. sign
27 Bro or sis
30 DDT target
33 A score
35 Pepsi-like
36 ???
37 Prepare (for)
38 "Giant" animals
40 Gets it, apparently
41 Microfilmer, maybe
42 Sportage maker
44 Antique show sign
45 Like this puzzle, when 36-Across is filled in
50 Your description of 36-Across
53 Wrest
54 Orthogonally moving piece
55 Pacific explorer
56 It's spotted in the West
57 Australia's Lake __
58 Test course obstacle
59 The "m" in m.o.
60 One who's not a procrastinator
61 Lingering effect
62 Responds peevishly

DOWN

1 Spread
2 Inspiration for poets and musicians
3 Appropriate dedication for this puzzle
4 Too popular
5 And not
6 Examine slyly
7 On the up and up
8 Congo forest dwellers
9 Duchamp works
10 Doctors call it parotitis
11 Met selection
12 Kind of sulfide
13 Renaissance family name
21 Old knife
22 Pitcher's change-up
24 Reply to a seat seeker
27 Minor setback
28 Septennial problem?
29 Tournament passes
30 Recipe abbr.
31 Trade
32 Counting-out word
34 Extensive knowledge
39 Hot, dry wind
40 The good earth?
43 At least equal
44 One who cleans drains
45 Hearth tool
46 Town near Bangor
47 Title locale in a 1937 Ronald Colman film
48 Devour
49 Waste
50 Wilbur's charge in 60's TV
51 Subject of a 1930's fad
52 "Don't stop"
56 U.K. leaders

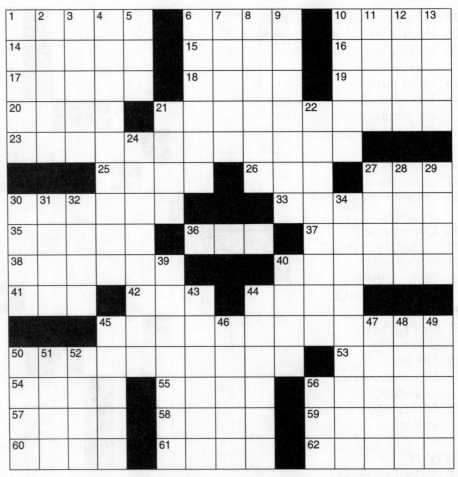

by Patrick Merrell   Thursday, November 29, 2001

SHORTZ SAYS:

Michael Shteyman emigrated from Russia to the United States just five years before this puzzle was published. At 17, he was one of the youngest constructors ever to have a puzzle in The Times. You would never know that English is his second language. This puzzle features a beautiful construction with eight theme answers.

ACROSS

1 Out-and-out
6 Door fastener
10 Drops in the morning?
13 Per __
14 Domed recess
15 French soul
16 Contract workers?
17 Campus V.I.P.
18 Whip but good
19 60's TV boy
20 Sneaky spy
23 Flat fees?
25 Sheik's guest, maybe
26 He was given the ears of a donkey, in myth
27 Like bad inflation
30 Grp. with its HQ in Brussels
31 Central street
32 Penalty declarer
34 __ Aviv
35 Inventor's desire
38 Texas border city
40 Messenger __
41 Roman 650
43 Measure (out)
44 "Diana" singer Paul
46 Molecular structure
51 Holiday songs
53 __ Moines
54 Think the world of
55 Jump-rope game
58 Break, financially
59 __ way (to some extent)
60 "My mistake!"
61 Familiar with
63 Comics outburst
64 Pro's rival
65 Land, as a fish
66 Washington and __ University
67 Clinton aide Panetta
68 __-slipper

DOWN

1 Chinese capital
2 Choosing
3 Speedy marching rate
4 Supped
5 Actress Turner
6 Rotter
7 Like some concerts
8 Future J.D.'s obstacle
9 Late breakfast hour
10 Four-person outing
11 Came forth
12 Left the band, perhaps
13 Musical combo?
21 Acquire
22 __ and tonic
24 Not sit
28 Abandon
29 Wire message
33 Jazz pianist Hines
35 Dinner-related
36 Proclaim
37 Look of surprise
39 Oboe, for one
42 Paved the way for
43 Catchall: Abbr.
45 Vodka or whiskey: Abbr.
47 Admits
48 So everyone can hear
49 Eye affliction
50 Arc lamp gas
52 School of fish
56 Through
57 Throw
62 Caribbean, e.g.

by Michael Shteyman

Tuesday, December 4, 2001

70

SHORTZ SAYS:
I don't believe in record-setting merely for the sake of record-setting. But this masterful construction both sets a record for the lowest number of entries (54) ever to appear in a standard 15x15-square grid and features lots of colorful vocabulary besides.

ACROSS
1 Boondocks
7 "The Virginian" writer
13 Dovetailed
15 Neighbor of Ciudad Juárez
16 Psychically
18 They may pull banners
19 Sole, e.g.
20 Log rollers?
21 Prisoner's desire
22 2001 French film comedy or its heroine
23 It may cover dark circles
24 Humorist __ Burgess of "purple cow" fame
25 Opposite of scarcity
27 Some queens' wear
31 Asking for a hand
32 Chocolate candy brand
33 Like some errors
40 Over-and-__ (two-barreled firearms)
41 Part of a one-sided tennis match
42 Gradually corrode
43 "Nanny and the Professor" family from 1970's TV
44 Kiwi, e.g.
45 Century in politics
46 Penitent
47 Optic screens
48 Mother __
49 Another shooting

DOWN
1 Choke
2 1956 U.S. figure skating gold medalist __ Albright
3 Ludicrous
4 Language descended from ancient Egyptian
5 Dangerous assailant
6 Amino acid in many proteins
7 Surfers' stops, perhaps
8 Black cats, supposedly
9 "Clockers" director, 1995
10 Feral
11 Beaux-__ (people with lively minds)
12 Tennis ace Marc
14 Scraps
17 "You've Really Got a Hold on Me" singers
26 Lost one's balance, perhaps
27 Lion or wolf
28 Blush
29 Gets under someone's skin?
30 Scary-sounding houseplant
31 Like oak leaves
32 Tot
34 Relatively regular
35 Give more stars to, maybe
36 Comment before "Ha, ha"
37 Williams title starter
38 Kind of station
39 Tenant

by Frank A. Longo

Saturday, December 15, 2001

SHORTZ SAYS:

This year-end puzzle features a theme of New Year's resolutions. Each theme answer is a familiar phrase reinterpreted in a punny way as someone's promise to do better the next year. The two constructors collaborated on this entirely by e-mail.

ACROSS

1 Pointed a pistol
6 Blockhead
10 Quantities: Abbr.
14 Mix-up
15 Nabisco cookie
16 Epitome of redness
17 Teetotaler's New Year resolution?
19 Cotton unit
20 Best guess: Abbr.
21 "__ Can" (Sammy Davis Jr. book)
22 French explorer La __
23 __-do-well
25 Comment of approval
28 Light touch
29 "Get lost!"
31 Bootlegger's New Year resolution?
33 Highlands hat
35 __ es Salaam
36 French girlfriend
37 Came in
41 "I'm a Believer" band, with "the"
43 Monopoly card
44 Singer's syllable
46 Born: Fr.
47 Executioner's New Year resolution?
50 Making sounds
54 Oils and watercolors
55 Lady-killers
57 Seward Peninsula city
58 All set
60 Pack away
62 __ Quentin
63 100-meter, e.g.
64 Scrabble player's New Year resolution?
67 Cruise stopover
68 Use a beeper
69 Donnybrook
70 Choreography move

71 Not barefoot
72 Has a need for Rogaine

DOWN

1 Trembling trees
2 Shortly
3 Guru
4 Flunking letters
5 Assigned task
6 Has some success
7 Circled the sun
8 Meadow
9 Bare peak
10 Palindromic pop group
11 When to eat
12 Fib
13 Places for church bells
18 Rooster's mate
22 60's radical org.
24 Family-friendly, in cinema
26 Smile widely
27 Cook's cover-up
30 Ruin
32 Hire
34 "Same here"
37 John Glenn player in "The Right Stuff"
38 Biblical lands
39 Octopus's arm
40 Bongo, for one
42 Carson City's state: Abbr.
45 Way back when
48 Have a go at
49 Greenhouse area
51 Sportscaster Howard
52 Dumbfounded
53 Telescope parts
56 "H-E-L-P!"
59 Hard to fathom
61 Embryo's site
64 Family M.D.'s
65 "Yay, team!"
66 __ culpa

by Nancy Salomon and Harvey Estes   Monday, December 31, 2001

72

SHORTZ SAYS:
Once again, here's proof that a crossword doesn't have to be hard to be exceptional. Besides the four basic theme answers in the longest spaces in the grid, look for four "bonus" theme-related entries in shorter spots.

ACROSS

1 "The Wizard of Oz" dog
5 __ Island (immigration point)
10 Birdbrain
14 On __ with (equal to)
15 Lasso loop
16 Decorative pitcher
17 Ten: Prefix
18 French fashion designer
20 Like bagpipes
22 First month in Madrid
23 Actress Skye
24 Emulate Salt-N-Pepa
26 Room with an easy chair
27 Spinning competition
31 How checks are signed
32 Regarding
33 __ de cologne
36 Litter members
37 Tropical ray
39 Islamic ruler
40 Road wiggle
41 King __
42 Ogling
43 1925 hit musical with the song "Tea for Two"
46 Lawn base
49 Letter after zeta
50 Bunches
51 Madison Square Garden, e.g.
53 Hearty breakfast
57 Performer in a cage
60 Historic periods
61 Med school subj.
62 Funny-car fuel
63 Quirks
64 Mediocre
65 Lip application
66 Cry from Santa

DOWN

1 Little ones
2 Oil grp.
3 __ Bell
4 They're given at graduations
5 Community next to Van Nuys
6 Ease up
7 __ Ness monster
8 Prefix with metric
9 Instant, for short
10 Student overseer
11 Had
12 Tractor maker John
13 Synthetic fabric
19 Aware of, slangily
21 Clock sound
24 Take five
25 "The Thin Man" canine
27 "Egad!"
28 Burden
29 Sounds made by 36-Across
30 Fancy ballroom steps
33 Give off
34 "__ She Sweet"
35 Impel
37 No longer worth debating
38 Ballerina Pavlova
39 Valuable things to give?
41 Work, as dough
42 Organic compound
44 Ones pointing fingers
45 Some Oldsmobiles
46 Long stories
47 Maine college town
48 "Le Viol" painter
52 Say __ (deny)
53 Eight: Prefix
54 Quartet minus one
55 R.p.m. indicator
56 Old Standard Oil brand
58 One of four for a square: Abbr.
59 Nothing

by Sarah Keller

Monday, January 28, 2002

SHORTZ SAYS:

Something you should know in order to solve this imaginative puzzle: In a letter bank, the letters of one word are used (and repeated as necessary) to spell a longer word or phrase. For example, IMPS is a letter bank of MISSISSIPPI.

ACROSS

1 Loudspeaker sound (and a letter bank for 60-Across)
6 Planets and such
10 Steamy
14 Howled
15 Raise a stink
16 Isaac's firstborn
17 See 71-Across
19 Hoosegow
20 Freshwater duck
21 Sporty Fords
23 What's more
27 Going strong
29 Became an issue
30 See 13-Down
33 Neigh-sayer
34 Educator Horace
35 Company with a dog in its logo
38 Applicable
41 Do away with
43 ___ Moines
44 Harmony
46 They have long tails
47 See 50-Down
50 Many states have them
53 Mrs. Chaplin
54 "___ Breckinridge"
55 Present from birth
57 Knock for a loop
59 Dutch cheese
60 See 1-Across
66 Queue
67 French cheese
68 Singer Abdul
69 Monopoly card
70 Sound
71 Ludicrous (and a letter bank for 17-Across)

DOWN

1 London's ___ 1 or ___ 2
2 "Love Story" composer Francis
3 "The Fountainhead" author Rand
4 VCR button
5 Touch up
6 More than fancy
7 Seeing things as they are
8 "Wanna ___?"
9 "Saturday Night Live" staple
10 It's often burning
11 Jeff Bagwell, notably
12 Hotel staff
13 Derby prize (and a letter bank for 30-Across)
18 Getting warm
22 Without exception
23 Orchard pest
24 Sierra ___
25 Lord's workers
26 Approximately
28 Ruler until 1917
31 Hang tough
32 Popular card game
35 Rootin'-tootin'
36 More adorable
37 Out of it
39 Dancer Charisse
40 Opposite of ecto-
42 Abound
45 Pen up
47 Made to take the fall
48 Main course
49 Spread (on)
50 Football locale (and a letter bank for 47-Across)
51 Actress MacDowell
52 Mindless
56 Goes back out
58 Vintner's valley
61 Pitcher's stat.
62 Skedaddled
63 Track feature
64 Ivy Leaguer
65 ___ Leman

by Greg Staples   Thursday, February 28, 2002

(74)

SHORTZ SAYS:
Many solvers completed this Patrick Berry puzzle without realizing what makes it an amazing feat of construction. Solve it, look carefully at your finished grid . . . and then be as astonished as I was when I first saw it.

ACROSS

1 To the extent that
8 Pebble-filled gourd
14 Sweet, dark wine
15 Inflexible
17 Spiritual leader of the Isma'ili Muslims
18 Rock band with a record-tying eight Grammys in 1999
19 Some babysitters
20 ⅛ of a fluid ounce
22 Suddenly lose it
23 Org.
24 Raft material
26 Skier McKinney
29 Marriage announcement
34 Place in which to luxuriate
37 "A __ plan . . ."
38 1981 miniseries set in ancient Israel
39 Theater passage
41 Where bottles of alcohol sit
42 Unmitigated
43 The Crimson Tide, familiarly
44 Influence on 1980's pop
45 Clorox or Clorets
46 Melon type
48 Strong supporter?
50 Booty
54 Fancy do
58 Fastener piece
59 "The Bell Jar" author
60 Dogsled runner, maybe
62 Martin Luther King Jr.'s birthplace
64 It's drained by traveling
65 Kigali resident
66 Lower limbs
67 Trumpet blast

DOWN

1 Appliance maker
2 They may span generations
3 Portrait painter __ Hals
4 With suspicion
5 Cheers
6 __ fin (at last): Fr.
7 Danger for a riverboat
8 "Mississippi __" (1992 film)
9 Portrait on an old 2¢ stamp
10 Succumbed to fear, maybe
11 Ledger entries: Abbr.
12 James of Hollywood
13 Tolstoy heroine
16 Pick
21 __ avis
25 Double platinum Genesis album of 1981
27 Actress Plummer
28 Brewer's need
30 Cry (for)
31 Captures
32 Can. borderer
33 __ Lee
34 Healing sign
35 One of Henry VIII's six
36 Name on a razor
38 Doll's utterance
40 Showing fatigue
41 One-fourth of a barbershop tune
43 Pastoral sounds
46 Noises from a rattletrap
47 Obliquely
49 Acknowledge
51 Fish in a John Cleese film
52 Perfume
53 Lake Volta's locale
54 Funny bit
55 "What a pity!"
56 Punishment for a pirate
57 Movie dog
59 Builder's need
61 Big 12 team: Abbr.
63 Old name in travel

by Patrick Berry   Thursday, March 21, 2002

SHORTZ SAYS:
This intricate and well-balanced puzzle contains multiple theme surprises. Crossword constructing doesn't get much better than this.

ACROSS

1 School of whales
4 Plowed layer
9 English of a sort
14 Ivy Leaguer
15 Controvert
16 Replay speed
17 Kind of garden
18 Cause winter isolation
19 Council Bluffs resident
20 Have a taste of
22 See 3-Down
24 Ted Williams was one
27 Governmental guarantee
31 It doesn't hold water
32 Delaware and Missouri
33 Encourage
36 This, in Toledo
38 Response to the Little Red Hen
39 Over there
40 Pink and lacy, perhaps
43 Egg carton abbr.
44 Bibliographic abbr.
46 Country that changed its name in 1939
47 Peace goddess
49 Attack from above
51 Irascible
53 Didn't heal well
54 Reactionaries, politically
58 1997 Fonda role
60 Spanish-speaking Muppet on "Sesame Street"
61 Composer Saint-__
64 "The speech of angels": Carlyle
67 "It's the __!"
68 Forelimb bones
69 How contracts are signed
70 Emissions-regulating org.
71 Like some 70's trousers
72 "Harry Potter" character Neville __
73 Marina del __

DOWN

1 Is stranded
2 Shake like __
3 With 22-Across, a Florida county
4 Star's demand
5 Break away
6 Corrida cry
7 Jr.'s namesake
8 Extend credit
9 Deck shoe
10 Potable in a fizz
11 Sound of impact
12 "__ ramblin' wreck . . ."
13 Oui's opposite
21 Change in Cuba
23 Chorus section
25 "If __ Would Leave You"
26 Move on the schedule
28 Quarters
29 Pretend
30 Set at the proper level, as a work force
33 "Look west," to a drill sergeant
34 Spike Lee's "She's __ Have It"
35 Growls
37 Bulova rival
41 Grenoble's river
42 Drop as low as possible
45 Having small gaps
48 Dark loaves
50 Feature of a smuggler's suitcase
52 Kind of bikini
55 Bannister, e.g.
56 Military camping spot
57 Pronto
59 Expressionist Nolde
61 Grinder
62 Pilsener kin
63 Blow-up: Abbr.
65 Game with Skip and Reverse cards
66 Confession topic

by Trip Payne

Thursday, April 4, 2002

"Brendan Quigley's crosswords are fresh, colorful, hip, and expertly constructed. He's one of the best puzzlemakers in *The New York Times*."

—Will Shortz, editor of the *New York Times* crossword puzzles

ENJOY THIS BONUS PUZZLE! *The New York Times Crossword All-Stars* features forty of Brendan Quigley's best *Times* puzzles, *plus* ten brand-new, never-before-published puzzles created especially for the book. Sharpen your pencil and dive in to this sneak-peek puzzle from *The New York Times Crossword All-Stars* book!

ACROSS

1 "Spare" items at a barbecue
5 Popular athletic shoes
10 Bullets and such
14 Melville tale
15 Beatle with a beat
16 Many a Seattle weather forecast
17 Classic pickup line #1
20 "Six Days, Seven Nights" co-star
21 Early night, to a poet
22 Permit: Abbr.
23 Prefix with -metric
24 Heavy hammer
27 Proofreader's mark
29 Not glossy, as a photo
32 Captain Morgan's drink
33 "Norma ___"
36 Dish served under glass
38 Classic pickup line #2
41 Geometric measurement
42 What Yahoo! searches, with "the"
43 Whichever
44 ___-off coupon
46 Mets stadium
50 Directs (to)
52 Ecol. watchdog
55 The "I" in T.G.I.F.
56 Prefix with skeleton
57 Numbers usually in parentheses
60 Classic pickup line #3
63 Pitcher
64 Genesis woman and namesakes
65 Allen of "Candid Camera"
66 Smart-mouthed
67 Cove
68 Fr. holy women

DOWN

1 Kansas City team
2 "Consider it done"
3 Dribble
4 Achy
5 City where van Gogh painted
6 Broadcasting giant
7 Ruler unit
8 Poet and novelist James
9 Michigan's ___ Canals
10 Napoleon led one
11 Wisconsin Avenue, in Georgetown
12 Opposite of max.
13 Washington's bill
18 ___ Beta Kappa
19 Let go of
24 Uncompromising
25 "Peter ___" of 50's–60's TV
26 Ambulance driver, for short
28 Car on rails
30 To the left, to sailors
31 Fri. preceder
34 Suffered humiliation
35 ___ Park, Colo.
37 Takes a chair
38 Soave, e.g.
39 Spring woe
40 Liking
41 Flag-waving org.
45 Churn
47 Went into seclusion
48 Endless, poetically
49 Liabilities' opposites
51 Put forth, as effort
53 ___ Blue Ribbon
54 Smashing point?
57 "You said it, brother!"
58 Sincere
59 Murders, slangily
60 Cool, once
61 Wonderment
62 ___ Lilly and Company

1

```
G O T   O V A L S   R A T S O
A N A   A I M E E   O T H E R
L E I   H O P O M Y T H U M B
L A W F U L   N I E C E
I T A L   C A S S   N A V E
C A N A S T A   H A C E K
  S T A R D A T E   L Y E
  S K I P T O M Y L O U
A L E   R E A S O N E R
P E R M S     R E N D E R S
T O F U   M A M E   E L A N
  P I E T A   H O R A C E
J U M P S T A R T E D   I K E
A G R E E   L I K E D   N E Z
W H I T E   L O O P S   E R E
```

2

```
O U T ↑   T M A N   H E N ↑
P L O W   R E C A P   I S I T
E M M A   A R E S O   A T C O
B R I N G D O W N T H E ↑
  M A C E   E A U
C L I N E   C U R B S I D E
A L A N S   H O T ↑ S   N O N
R A N G   H A N E S   S E N D
T R I   S O R T S   O P E N ↑
↑ A N D H O M E   G L I D E
  E E K   B R A T
↑ O F B L U E L E A V E S
C I A O   P A U L S   F U N ↑
A S S N   S C A L P   U V E A
T E T E   H U E S   L A D D
```

3

```
I B M   D O C   S T L E O
V E R D A N T   S T E A R N S
S E N O R E S   T U M B R E L
  P O P I N   W A F   A C E
S E V E N D W A R F S   T H E
P R A Y   H S T   E Q U I P
A S K   U T E P   G R U M P Y
  S N O W W H I T E
S N E E Z Y   A Y L A   F E W
H O S N I   D I P   H I Y A
R P I   P O I S O N L A D E N
U L A   R A T   T Y P E B
B A S H F U L   T E M P L A R
S C O R E R S   E S P Y I N G
  E N E R O   N T H   O K S
```

4

```
C U R A T E S   H G W E L L S
E T A G E R E   E L A T I O N
E N T R A N T   L O Y A L T Y
S E A   R E O   I S O L A T E
  B O S N S   S U I
A U G U S T   K R A T I O N S
S N O R E   H A I R   L O T
A R A B   W I T T Y   D I N O
N I L   I D E A   C O V E N
A G L I T T E R   N E G A T E
  N E H   S P I N S
A C C O R D S   A C T   T I M
D O O V E R S   U K R A I N E
A M M E T E R   L E A S E R S
H E B R E W S   A L L U R E S
```

5

```
              P
P G A   S H O U T S   B A C K
E R S   H O R N E T   O B O E
R O S   A L E X E I   O N M E
D U O   M E L S   R A K E I N
U N C A P   S U M   C I R C E
  D I D O   E T U D E S
S H A D O W   A L E   H E W N
P O T   S I X W E E K   L O U
A G E S   R M N   M A R M O T
  P A Y E E S   R O O D
H A Z E L   N Y E   L O R C A
A D O N I S   P R O S   O H M
D O R S   T S H I R T   P U T
A B B E   O R I A N A   E C O
T E A R   P O L L E D   R K O
```

6

```
  T O P J O B   L E A S T
M E R C U R Y   M Y L A R S
S T E P P E R   N E P T U N E
G E M   I G O T   S A U D I S
  S T O N E D   C R Y P T
M A R T E N   L O G A N
A D E E R   V E N U S   A B A
R E N T   N E S T S   O R A L
S S E   S Y N C S   E V O K E
  P L U T O   U R A N U S
M A M I E   S P I N A L
P L A N E T   E N D S   B A A
S T R A P I N   C O I N I N G
I N T E N T   A N N E T T E
E A R T H   N E G A T E
```

7

```
KOS . ABODE . MBA
RATE MORAY . JOEL
UTES ICAME ARGO
PERSONALPRONOUN
ARNEB . PENNE
. BLT . HUH .
TROLLER ENTWINE
SURVIVE ACHATES
PERIGEE PLANETS
. ARS . SEL .
ASSET . MALAY
SYMBOLFORIODINE
CRIB ALGER ETNA
AITS SARTO SUES
PAH . TWEEN . PET
```

8

```
AREA PAWN SANTA
BANG ALAI CLEON
ADEN PELT HIVED
COMEBACKSHANE
ANYWAY OVERDO
. NAILERS MAD
LIST SIBS LONE
FAMOUSLASTWORDS
ISMS PANE HUEY
SSE ROMANIA
HOLIER DROPIT
. THATSALLFOLKS
ARIEL AMIE NANA
BANAL VEER ATOR
ANGRY ENDS SEWS
```

 9

```
SUPRA AMMO ROOF
APSES DAIS ERMA
TRYST SUSPICION
RICTAL VERTIGO
ASH OVEREAT
PEONAGE SYNERGY
. BAIRD BEE
HITCHCOCKMOVIES
OFA LIANE
SIDEBAR TREEFUL
LORELEI RNA
REBECCA SANEST
NOTORIOUS RANEE
AVOW NIDI ADZES
PENS GLEN MAYNT
```

 10

```
TRIBE DALI CLAM
OOZED EBAN RACE
GOODINVESTMENTS
ODD FOIL RADISH
PITT TORI
MALICIOUSINTENT
ANISE NATE QUI
DIVA HAIRS BURN
ATE MEMO SOUSE
MARKEDINCREASES
EDGE AUNT
SORTIE ERIE RAJ
WRETCHEDINGRATE
ANIL OVEN ADMIT
GENE GANG LASTS
```

 11

```
PAPA EDGAR CAFE
OLIN VERNE USER
MICE IREAD THEA
PICNIC GREATEST
ADATE MYTH
AND NITE EARNA
LOIS OATH LOOSE
FILLINTHEBLANKS
ARLES SERA TOMS
EYEOF LENO NEE
PULP ISLES
TELLTALE HELENS
ERIE MATTE INON
AGES ENTRE ASTI
MOSS STAYS SEAT
```

 12

```
ICALL LOSTASTEP
MEDEA ATLIBERTY
PROGNOSTICATION
AIL ALSOP STONE
ISPY DOM BEE
REHAB SAFE RAZZ
RIB NORM POE
[CLINTON/BOBDOLE] ELECTED
AUR SARA ERR
TIAS SASH VALOR
AIT PAS BARA
AWARD EERIE MAP
MISTERPRESIDENT
OSTRACISM RINGO
SHOELACES ENTER
```

*Two possible answers fit 39-Across

13

```
S W A G S   S C U P   C R O C
A P L E A   E R N E   H E R O
M A L T L I Q U O R   I T E M
  U N T R U E   M E N A G E
D E V O   M E L T I N G P O T
A R I   B A L   O T T   E N O
G A U Z E   E M M E T
  M I L T O N B E R L E
  P A R E D   E C L A T
I R E   T A I   A D D   O L E
M O L T E N L A V A   U N I T
B O U N D S   B A L I N G
I N D O   M U L T I G R A I N
B E E T   I D E A   O U T R E
E Y R E   T E R R   R H E T T
```

14

```
H O I S T S   I H A D   J A B
M A N T R A   N A V E   A D O
O R D A I N   T I G E R C U B
  I R K   P E T   P O K E S
B R A V E M A R I N E R
L U N E   O Y L   E N E R O
A B E D   V I E   E D M O N D
S I X   R E N A R D S   Y E R
T E P E E S   G A L   M A D E
  S O T T O   U T E   A L G A
  Y A N K E E D O D G E R
S W A M I   N P R   V I I
M E T A N G E L   C A S A B A
E R A   E L L A   A T O N A L
W E D   R O L Y   T E N T H S
```

15

```
C O E D   S H I P   A D L I B
H A L E   P O K E   T R A D E
I T S A   O V E N   V I R A L
C H E R K N E   E C H O
  Y G R F I T H S H O W
D I V I D E   A M B I T
E M I R   S T P A T   G A S
J P E A N U T T E R S W I C H
A S S   E M A I L   E R M A
  T S A R S   T A B L E D
B E A V I S T H E A D
O L D S   N O S S O R S
A I D E S   Y E T I   E X I T
S T E T S   A G E S   M E S A
T E R S E   W O R M   I N K Y
```

* The theme answers are (but)CHER KN(if)E, (and)Y GR(if)ITH
SHOW, J(if) PEANUT (but)TER S(and)WICH, BEAVIS (and)
(but)T-HEAD, and NO (if)S (and)S OR (but)S.

16

```
G A L S   C A V E R   P E T S
A L O E   A D I E U   E X I T
T O S C A   R O B E R T   T U T O R
R O O S T E R S   B E L L E
  H O S E   S M A R T E D
A S S E T S   S T A B S
S E A L   A H O L E   A R T
H A M L E T S O L I L O Q U Y
E N E   L I T R E   R U S K
  A G R E E   S E D A T E
D E C R I E R   M A G I
E L L E N   S A Y O N A R A
N O T I O N   A C T O R S   A D O B E
E T N A   F O R T S   L I S A
S E E S   T O K Y O   S T E M
```

17

```
D A T A   A S K S   A C H E D
E T A T   R A I L   B O O L A
F A I T H G I L A   S P L A T
A L G A E   N O M S   P Y L E
T E A C A R T   S A B O T
  K R U P A   W A L E S A
D A W S   L I M P   B A R M Y
E V E   D E T A I L S   R U E
B O I T O   A N A T   G A G S
I N G R I D   A N D S O
  H I T U P   O S T O S I S
S W A G   B E S T   E D I C T
K A N G A   S T U D P O L K A
I N K E D   T O N E   N O E L
P E A R S   S W A B   E S S E
```

18

```
D I S C S   F A Z E   X V I
A C H O O   A M E N   Q U I Z
D O U B L E X I N G   A P S O
A N T   V I E D   R A T T E D
  L E N D   S A R A H
M A X I N E   R E V E R E N T
O N S E T   M A G E S   B A R
P I P S   C O L O R   J A V A
E S E   I H O P S   C A N E D
D E E P D I S H   P A D D L E
  D R O N E   L Y R E
F I B U L A   A U R A   O H O
A V I D   S I G N O F T H E X
R A K E   E T R E   E R N I E
O N E   A S I S   S W O R N
```

19

```
S O C K E T ▪ A S P I S H ▪
T H R I V E ▪ P H A N T O M ▪
A B A T E R ▪ L I S T E N E D
G O V E R N M E N T ▪ M E T A
E Y E S ▪ ▪ A N N E X ▪ S C I
▪ ▪ M O N T Y ▪ F E T A S
▪ S C U L L Y ▪ V I R I L E
F A T A L L Y ▪ B E L I E F S
O R E I D A ▪ A L I E N S ▪
S C E N E ▪ S P I N S ▪ ▪
S A P ▪ R A N T S ▪ W R A P
E D E N ▪ C O N S P I R A C Y
S I N E C U R E ▪ E D I T O R
▪ A E R A T E S ▪ R E T I R E
▪ D O P E R S ▪ M A S O N S
```

20

```
C A H N ▪ A L F A ▪ ▪ C H I N
O L I O ▪ B I L L G ▪ A I M E
S O L S ▪ E M I L Y ▪ S F P D
M O D E S T P R O P O S A L ▪
O F A G E ▪ S T Y ▪ N I L E S
▪ ▪ A A A ▪ R E S U M E
I S P Y ▪ S H A V E N ▪ T E D
T H I S D I A M O N D R I N G
H A L ▪ R A T T L E ▪ A N T E
O R E G O N ▪ ▪ W A N ▪
T E D I O ▪ R B I ▪ P A T S Y
▪ W I L L Y O U M A R R Y M E
M I N D ▪ E L O P E ▪ I R O N
E T T E ▪ S L Y E R ▪ S O R T
S H O D ▪ O S L O ▪ K L E E
```

21

```
W R A P S ▪ F L A T ▪ S ♥ I T
H O R A E ▪ S U R E ▪ S C A R
O U I J A ▪ ♥ T E N ▪ R O M E
A T L A S T ▪ E A T S ▪ A B E
▪ ▪ M O E T ▪ S H O R T S ♥
C I L A N T R O ▪ S A Y ▪ ▪
L A P ♥ ▪ R O N A ▪ R E C A P
E G G ▪ A U ♥ S Y ▪ A H A
F O A M Y ▪ T O N E ▪ ♥ P E R
▪ ▪ B A R ▪ F E A R S O M E
♥ D R A W E R ▪ R H E E ▪ ▪
S A O ▪ N C A A ▪ S I C K E N
I Z O D ▪ T I P ♥ ▪ G R I P E
D E F T ▪ O T I S ▪ N E W E R
E S ♥ S ▪ S T A Y ▪ S T I E D
```

22

```
B R I D A L ▪ A R M O I R E ▪
A E R A T E ▪ C H E S T E R ▪
A M A Z O N ▪ S E T H O M A S
▪ ▪ E M I T ▪ N E A ▪ A S P
A C H ▪ N O S I R ▪ B I E R
R H O D A ▪ U S S ▪ W E N D Y
G E O R G E R S H W I N ▪
O R D A I N ▪ ▪ O L D I E S
▪ ▪ P L A C I D O M I N G O
O H G E E ▪ A D O ▪ A X I O M
L E A D ▪ S T A F F ▪ T S E
E L I ▪ S A C ▪ F A T E ▪
G E N E W M A N ▪ R I D G E D
▪ N O T A B L E ▪ E L N I N O
A N O M A L Y ▪ S T A N D S
```

23

```
S P A C E D ▪ M A C A D A M S
A R C H I E ▪ A L U M I N U M
T I T A N I C S T R U G G L E
▪ C U T ▪ G A T E S ▪ E L L
P E A ▪ E N T I R E ▪ A L I T
A T L A N T I C S A L M O N ▪
R A L S T O N ▪ ▪ T O O ▪
▪ G Y P O ▪ ▪ ▪ C U B S
▪ ▪ R M S ▪ S T A N L E Y
▪ I C E B E R G L E T T U C E
K L E E ▪ D E N U D E ▪ E T S
U L A ▪ A D A G E ▪ A N O
D I S A S T E R S U P P O R T
O N E W H E E L ▪ M O S S E R
S I D E A R M S ▪ S P E E D Y
```

24

```
R E I N ▪ S A T E ▪ ▪ R U B E
A R T Y ▪ E X I L E ▪ A L A N
B A S E B A L L I N F I E L D
E T A ▪ A L E E ▪ C O S E T S
▪ ▪ I C I ▪ S A R I ▪
P E R S O N W H O S U N H I P
A L I E N ▪ H A R E M ▪ A R A
T I G E ▪ G I S T S ▪ E G A N
H H H ▪ L O T T O ▪ A C U T E
O U T S I D E O F A W H E E L
▪ ▪ A L L Y ▪ L O O ▪ ▪
H A S S L E ▪ A M O K ▪ A C T
O R C H E S T R A M E M B E R
A G U A ▪ S A N T A ▪ A B L E
R O M Y ▪ J E E R ▪ W A L K
```

25

```
S T E M . C L O Y . . J A K E
L O D I . R A V E S . E M I T
E N G A G E M E N T S T O N E
W E E . O P E N . A P H I D S
. . . A L E . . B R E R . . .
E V E N A S A N A C C O U N T
M E L O N . B A T H S . T O O
A R I D . A N N O Y . N I N A
I D O . G L E N N . S O L E D
L I T E R A R Y S O C I E T Y
. . G E M S . . P H R . . . .
S T E R E O . S E E M . A L F
L O V E R S I M B R O G L I O
U K E S . A C U R A . A P E X
M E S S . . E G O S . B O N Y
```

26

```
M A S T E R S E R G E A N T S
I N T H E L I N E O F F I R E
A G A I N S T T H E G R A I N
S U N N Y . T R A S H . G P S
M I L K . L I E U T . F A L A
I S E . N I G E L . B E R E T
C H E E T A H S . B O R A T E
. . . P E R T . M O O R . . .
R E M I S S . G I U L I A N I
E R E C T . C E S T A . L A M
B E T S . G A L E S . R A S P
E W E . L A M A R . C I S C O
C H O C O L A T E S H A K E S
C O U N T E R I R R I T A N T
A N T S I N O N E S P A N T S
```

27

```
B A G S . M U T T . . N E A P
U N I T . A H O S T . U R G E
T E L E . N O R A H . T O A T
. W A I T T H E R E S M O R E
. . N O R . . R O E . . . . .
M A K E S A G R E A T G I F T
A D A M S . R A M P S . D A W
C A R . . B I D D Y . L V I
O N A . G E N I E . S T E R N
N O T S O L D I N S T O R E S
. . A L L . . E A R . . . . .
A N D I F Y O U A C T N O W
Q U A G . U N C L E . A J A X
U N D O . P O L E D . D A L I
A S S N . . R A C E . O I L S
```

28

```
E U R E K A C A . A M U S E D
T H E M A T I C . N O N U S E
E U G E N E O R . E R I E P A
S H O E . . E M M A . S Y N
. . R A N G . D I N K . .
M I A . E A U C L A I R E W I
A B N O R M A L . S A L E M
Y S E R . E M A I L . F L E A
B E G A N . R O A S T I N G
E N G L E W O O D C O . E Y E
. . S W A N . E T U I . .
M A W . B L O C . C O S A
E N I D O K . E D I S O N N J
G A L O R E . D E M E N T I A
A T T E N D . E L P A S O T X
```

29

```
B I S E C T O R . S H A L O M
A L P A C I N O . T I R A N A
L E A R N E D T H E R O P E S
E A R L Y R E T I R E M E N T
. . . . . E M E R A L D S
L O G C A B I N . . . . . .
A D L A I E S T E V E N S O N
D O U B L E S O L I T A I R E
D R E S S T O T H E N I N E S
. . . . . . H I D A L G O S
S N U B N O S E . . . . .
C O L L E G E C A M P U S E S
A C T I V E V O L C A N O E S
M A R N I E . R E C L I N E R
P L A I N S . E X C E S S E S
```

30

```
H A M . H O D . . C A N A R Y
O M A . A J A M . O P A Q U E
M A C A R O N I . D A V I E S
I Z A A K . I N F E R . . .
N E W S . F E D E X . G O T O
G D S . C A L M S . Y O K E L
. . . H O L L Y . S O U R E D
. T R I P L E P A N G R A M .
J A U N T S . S Q U I D . .
E X I T S . D A U B S . D I A
W I N S . J O N A S . W O O L
. . L E N D L . T O O N E
O R A T O R . Q U I C K F I X
R E V I V E . S N O B . U Z I
I B A N E Z . G U Y . S E A
```

31

```
A G A P E   A N A P   N E S T
S I D E D   P O L E   A S E A
K R O N A   A T A N   S T A G
A D R A M A C R I T I C I S
N E E     S E E N   M A M I E
T R E B E K       P R A D O
    S E E S T O     T E N
  A M A N W H O L E A V E S
F L O   H E A R S E
E L V E S     N E X T T O
W I E S T   A L O E   O E R
  N O T U R N U N S T O N E D
S A N E   O N C E   R H I N E
A L T E     W E I R   I N T E R
G L O M   E X E S   G O E R S
```

32

```
P A P A   S T A T   L O C I
O L A V   P U M A   P U P A L
S L Y A S A F O X   A T A L L
I O U   A R T S   S W I L L S
T Y P I S T     T O P S
    S H A R P A S A T A C K
A D A M   N A R R O W   L O O
V O W S   D I T   S A I L
I D O   A N I M A L   A N N A
S O L I D A S A R O C K
    G A S H   Q U I L T S
A B R U P T   H O U R   A H A
B L O A T   F A T A S A P I G
B O O N S   A L I T   M I C A
A T T A   R O S S   A S K S
```

* This crossword has no E's in either the answers or the clues.

33

```
S S T   F I N E R   S T A L L
A T E   A M O R E   I O N I C
H O P   I F N O M I N A T E D
I W I L L   P O I S E D
B E D E L I A   T I C   L A G
    N E A R S   T U P E L O
A N A T   G E A R   R U N T O
M E X I C O I F E L E C T E D
I W I L L   L E T O   C O R E
L E A S E S   S U S H I
E L L   A H A   R E E N A C T
  O N E M A N   F I G H T
E X T R A D I T I O N   L O O
V I N C I   S E N S E   E S P
A S T A R   S E G E R   Y E S
```

34

```
S P U R   A M O S   C H A M P
W I N E   L E A H   A I M E E
A L D A   A L T O   N E A R S
Y O U C A N T H O L D   N E T
S T E T S   S T E I N
    T A R   S I D E O N E
A S S U A G E S   S E E S I N
D O W N   I F Y O U   D O N T
A R A F A T   M O R A S S E S
S E M I N A L   H E M
    T O T E S   A S T R O
O S S   D O W N W I T H H I M
P A T S Y   D I E D   I O T A
A G A I N   E P E E   E L A N
L E Y T E   R E D S   D E S I
```

35

```
P A R I S   A F B   L A P E L
A L O N E   C A L   I R A T E
L E T S G E T Q U A C K I N G
  S E A M S   S I D E   L A O
    N E T S   S O N S
V O T E N E I G H   S E R B S
I R A   T E T E   B E T H E L
T O U R   M E E S E   S O Y A
A N N A L S   N E A R   M O N
L O T T O   B A A H U M B U G
    A B L E   L E N O
A D A   B E A U   R A M P S
W I L L Y O U S H O W M E O W
L E V E E   T E A   A I S L E
S T A I R   Y R S   Y E T I S
```

36

```
C R A G   B R A   S I C K O
H U G O   O A T   D U N L A P
A N A C O N D A   R E 3 I N E
M A M A S   I N T E R I M
O W E R S   A D V I S A B L E
I A 6 T   A N T S   N E I N
S Y N   R I C O   S E C R E T
    T E L E P H O N E
G O B O T S   E O N S   H I S
E C R U   A R U G   C O N E
L A U 4 N G G A S   E R N S T
  I T E R A T E   L 2 O A T
D E S O T O   O C U L A R L Y
A L E U T S   R A E   K E E P
D I R T Y   S T Y   E R S E
```

On a telephone, 2=ABC, 3=DEF, 4=GHI, 6=MNO

37

```
A L I A S | C O M E | S H O P
L E O N E | A P I A | W A D E
A C T I N | R A N T | A V O W
W H A T D O P R I S O N E R S
      | R E L E T | A N D |
S A H A R A | S T A I N E R
A G E | F R A T | I V A N A
R O A R S | U S E | R E N D S
A G R E E | I S M S | C A P
N O N A G O N | U P S E T S
      | R A W | R I C H E |
T O C A L L E A C H O T H E R
A M E X | E R N E | O T E R O
C O O L | T A D A | E E R I E
H O S E | S T Y X | Y E S E S
```

*Answer to riddle: CELL PHONES

38

```
A V E R S | C A S E | S P A T
L E G I T | A M E N | H A S H
L E G G E D R A C E | E S S O
    | S P I L T | A L T A R
T H O U | P O I N T P L A Y
H E L P S | A R E A |
R A E | A R C H I E | C O L D
E R A | W H E E L E R | R A F
E T N A | O D E S S A | A M I
    | D A D E | M O T E L
  | P I E C E S U I T | P E R M
G R O P E | L A I N E |
A I N T | R I N G C I R C U S
S O I L | C I A O | N A O M I
P R A Y | A I R S | A S T A R
```

39

```
D T S | R I O T | N U R S I E
R I M | O N M E | U G A N D A
A B A | S P A N I S H M A I N
F I L M C A R D S | J I G
T A L L O W | M O D E L
  | V E N O M | N U T M E G
S I S I | D I A N E | A L I
I C U | T H E S P O T | I L L
L E G | H E D D A | S L E D
T R A V E L | O R N A N
  | R I A L S | A D A G E S
  | A B R | S C A P E G O A T
T R E A S U R E M A P | O R E
O M E G A S | L I L T | F L A
E S T O P S | L E M S | S Y D
```

40

```
A R T S | B A S I C | S T A G
L U A U | A M O C O | A H M E
I N R E | Y E M E N | D E B T
B O Z | H O N E | T R A V I S
A V A L O N | B E A U T I E S
B E N I C E | O L I N | I N E
A R T E | T I D I N G | I T T
  | H U M | S Y D | S C I
A B E | I M A G E S | R I I S
T R A | D E A R | E L A I N E
T A P D A N C E | C A G I E R
E V E R S O | A W R Y | I R V
M E M O | R O S I E | L I R A
P L A N | A L E R T | A N O N
T Y N E | H A D E S | B E R T
```

41

```
P H I L I P S | R A R E B I T
R A N A T E M P E R A T U R E
O U T S I D E A G I T A T O R
F L I T S | L E E D S | T N N
I S M S | P L A N E | L O M A
L I A | P A I N T | M A N E T
E N T W I N E S | M A X E N E
  | E A G E R | B A Y E D
P S A L M S | M A C A R O N I
A P P L Y | S I Z E S | N O G
R O P Y | R A M O S | M E I N
A K A | H E L I O | L A S S O
G A R R I S O N K E I L L O R
O N E T H I N G A T A T I M E
N E L S O N S | S C R A P E D
```

42

```
A B O L I S H | A L S O R A N
T O R O N T O | D E C L A R E
E A S Y C O M E E A S Y G O
E T O | L I E N | R E C O N
  | C U I N G | P E N H |
S A C H S | G O U R D | A M O
C L O U D S | S S E | D R A B
H E R M A N M E L V I L L E
M A N S | I C U | L I V E L Y
O F F | S T I N G | C A S E S
  | I C E S | T A L E S |
I H E A R | O O Z E | G A P
S I L V E R M E D A L I S T
A D D E N D A | B O L I V I A
Y E S D E A R | O N E N E S S
```

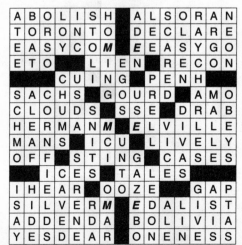

43

```
T T T T   T T T T   T T T T T
T H A R   H I H O   O R O U T
T Y K E   O R E M   T A I N T
T M E N   N A S A   I N L E T
T E N D S   D U T I E S
      S T E P O N   I M I T
T A L K T O   R E C   E A S T
T R I E S O N E S H A N D A T
T A P E   K I M   E X T E N T
T B S P   I N E S S E
      S E N E C A   L I G H T
T A M A R   S O W S   N E E T
T R I T E   P U P S   E T A T
T U N I C   O R I G   P A R T
T T T T   T T T T   T T T T
```

44

```
B E T T E   P E T     M A A M
R U R A L   A W E   H A S T A
E R I C A   L E X L U T H O R
T O M K I T E   T E N C E N T
      N E S S   N T H
A N G L E D   L O A F   S P A
S E R I F   H A R P O   T A N
T H E D E C E M B E R K I N G
E R E   B R I M S   R A N D R
R U N   R A R E   B E N G A Y
      M U D   R O A D
U N S E A L S   U N J A D E D
N E W S R E E L S   U S U R Y
D A I S Y   N E T   L I L L E
O R G Y   D O S   Y A L E S
```

45

```
P U P   F L A K   E P O C H S
E N E   R O S A   S O W H A T
A D R O I T L Y   S I E R R A
S O U P   S O A P   S O A R
      T H A N K E R   M S T
M E N S A   G E T A C R O S S
A R I   B O A R   B O A S
Y A M M E R S   D I S P O S E
  B I A S   B I N S   M I A
B U L L S E Y E S   E V E N T
I V E   R E Q U I T E
B U N S   N U N S   N U T S
B L E E P S   E I N S T E I N
E A S E L S   S T O W   L E A
D E S P O T   T E T E   E R G
```

46

```
S U M P   A T A L L   S T L O
A L A R   J U N I O   T E A L
I N R E   A B O V E B O A R D
D A Y C A R E   B O A R D
A S S A Y   S I S I
      U N O P E N   T A N I A
L A S T   N E X T T O L A S T
A L A I   M A T E O   O P I A
B E F O R E H A N D   H A N D
S C E N E   E N D O R A
      F O N T   A S C A P
  M I N E S   B E D T I M E
U N D E R M I N E S   A G A R
S O L E   A D U L T   T A T E
A P E D   N O B L E   E R I S
```

47

```
B E A   R A W E S T   L I T
E N D   E X A R C H   M O N O
H B O   B E G G A R   A S H E
A L L S   N O B I G D E A L
N O P L A C E   S C U T T L E
  C H I M E R A   E N V I E S
    N O D I C E   M R S
    N O G R E A T S H A K E S
C O P   N O S A L E
A T E S T S   R E L A Y E D
P I N H E A D   N O N U K E S
N O C O N T E S T   P E S O
U N I T   I C K I E R   O I L
T A T S   R O Y A L E   U R I
S L Y   E Y E L I D   T E D
```

48

```
U N T O   R A N D O M   M U D
S E R F   I L O I L O   A R Y
D R A F T D O D G E R   R B I
A D M   H E F   A I D A N
      D I R T Y D A N C I N G
D E M O N S   O L D I E
U S A G E   D I E S D O W N
A S I S   T H E I N   T R A C
D O N E D E A L   T E T R A
  A R N I E   M I A S M A
D E R R I N G D O E R S
A R I S E   I R E   A U S
D O T   D O U B L E D U T C H
D D E   U N P E E L   N A L A
Y E S   P A S T R Y   D D A Y
```

49

```
L E F T . C A B L E . T R E E
A L I E . O L E O S . O A K S
N E D S . M O N O P L A N E S
E C O T Y P E S . I O D I D E
. . A M A . S E A . . . . . .
H E R M A N N . N S F . R E D
E R I E . Y O G A . E P O D E
S W A N S . W O K . R E V U E
S I L T Y . A B E L . R E C D
E N S . S O I . S A T I R E S
. . T N T . P A S . . . . . .
E A S T E R . S H O O T I N G
G R A Y M A T T E R . Y S E R
G U N K . M E A N T . L E I A
S M E E . P A R S E . E E L S
```

50

```
C L O S E S I N . L A I R . .
A I R P L A N E . A R C E D .
L E W I S O F P O P M U S I C
A D E L E . A H Y E S . O V A
I T L L . S M E L L . C L E M
S O L . S T O W S . S O U S E
. . H A U S . S C O T I A . .
T R U M A N S O P P O N E N T
R O N A L D . F R E T . . . .
A L F I E . E D I C T . G N P
G L O M . F L O S S . B L U R
I S R . D R A N O . R O O T Y
C O M I C A L A N D E R S O N
. N E R V Y . L E A V E S I N
. D A I S . D R Y S D A L E .
```

51

```
B L A N K E T P O L I C I E S
N A T I O N A L H O L I D A Y
A I R C O N D I T I O N E R S
I D I E . I A G O . C A N T .
. . R O S H . E C H . . . . .
S T A K E . T A X I . J A N .
E S C A L A T O R C L A U S E
G A R R I S O N K E I L L O R
A D E L A I D E S L A M E N T
R I D . N C O S . T A P E S .
. . P T S . T A M E . . . . .
A C N E . B R N O . D R U M .
T H E D E T R O I T L I O N S
Y O U R F E E T S T O O B I G
A C R O S S T H E S T R E E T
```

52

```
S T A M P . I L S A . A X L E
E R R O R . C U L L . T R E X
M E T R O P O L I S . R A N T
S K Y . P I N U P . S A Y S O
. . C H E(S)(S)E T . V E L .
P E K O E(S) . (S)O L I D S
C A R A T . (S)T E P P E S .
S T Y X . W A(S)I N . G I G I
. P E T I T E(S) . P R O U D
A S T R O(S) . (S)E E N T O
T A O . L E(S)(S)U R E . .
L I N E D . N E H R U . E S S
A L I A . M A N O F S T E E L
S O T S . I R O N . E A R L E
T R E Y . G E R E . S C O L D
```

53

```
C A S H C O W . G A V E L S .
A P P E A S E . T H E I D E A
W E L L S E T . R E S T U F F
E M I L E . S C O T . A C T E
D E C O D E . O U T . L A B S
. N E D . T O P T O P . T A T
. . O Z O N E . A T O N . . .
. A L L I N A D A S W O R K .
. M I L T . I C O N O . . . .
N E T . S L A T E D . T E C .
O R T S . O H O . A S H C A N
W I L E . V E R B . I F A L L
I C E D T E A . E N G A R D E
S A M E O L D . L I M I T E R
E N E R G Y . S T A R E R S .
```

54

```
I B A R S . A H S O . A J A R
T E V Y E . N O I R . L O C O
S L E E π N G π L L . C H A P
E A R . A O L . L E M O N D E
L I S A . E E C . A B A S E .
F R E N χ N D O χ N A . U M A
. G A D . U P S . I ν I T .
S O φ S T . L P S . A N ν A L
K I L T . H A D . F L A . .
A L A . V E G η B L η L L O W
. C D R O M . T O O . L O L A
W O E I S M E . N O S . O D D
I L L S . E D μ N D μ S K I E
S O φ E . R I L E . R A T E R
E R A S . S T E T . F L O S S
```

55

```
H A ─ O T A T ▮ ▮ P O L K A ●
E P I T A P H S ▮ O R I O L E
M O N T R E A L ▮ K E N N E L
P P G ▮ R E L O S E ▮ E A R L
▮ ─ I K I ▮ P R I M ▮ ▮ ▮
▮ S M E E ▮ A H A ▮ P E R I ●
▮ T A R D E ▮ O N E O N O N E
R O M ▮ M O R S E ▮ ▮ W E D
E L I S I O N S ▮ L A G E R
─ I E L L ▮ T E A ▮ D O L T
▮ ▮ I S A W ▮ T H E ● ▮ ▮
M E A D ▮ B O A T E L ▮ B A G
A L B I N O ▮ M I L I T A T E
D A R N E R ▮ S C E N A R I O
─ L I G H T ▮ ▮ A N E C ● E S
```

56

```
P O L I T I C A L S Y S T E M
O V E R I M A G I N A T I V E
M E A T T H E R M O M E T E R
E R R ▮ T E N O N ▮ M A H R E
R E N T E R S ▮ O M E L E T S
A M E E R S ▮ S L U R S ▮ ▮
N O D E S ▮ L O O T S ▮ B I B
I T O N ▮ B A D G E ▮ B A M A
A E F ▮ C A D D Y ▮ W A S P S
▮ ▮ P O B O Y ▮ L I N E R S
V A P O R E D ▮ T A L K S U P
C L A S S ▮ G A R T H ▮ E D A
H O S T I L E T A K E O V E R
I N S E C T R E P E L L E N T
P E E R A S S E S S M E N T S
```

57

```
C A E N ▮ ▮ P A S O ▮ P R O S
O G L E ▮ C @ C H P H R A S E
Q U A D R @ I C E Q U @ I O N
▮ A L B I N O ▮ ▮ H E L L O
▮ ▮ E P A ▮ R O B ▮ R @ E R
T R E @ ▮ P E @ B O G S ▮ ▮
S O F T C ▮ N @ T E R ▮ A R M
P O L Y U N S @ U R @ E D F @
S K @ ▮ G O U T S ▮ E X U D E
▮ ▮ M @ U R @ E S ▮ P E S O
M O T A ▮ N E S ▮ E T @ ▮ ▮
A G E N T ▮ ▮ S T E R N O ▮
G R E @ E X P E C T @ I O N S
D E T E R I O R @ E ▮ @ R E E
A S H E ▮ S W @ S ▮ ▮ E I L @
```

58

```
T W O S ▮ R O T O S ▮ E D A M
A R N E ▮ A D U L T ▮ U R S A
R I L E ▮ N O B L E ▮ R U N T
S T O R M D R A I N S ▮ N E T
A H A ▮ A I S L E ▮ L A K E R
L E N O X ▮ ▮ P A R A D E
▮ ▮ B I C Y C L E T I R E S
M O S E ▮ L E H A R ▮ O D D S
A R M Y F A T I G U E S ▮ ▮
S P E E D Y ▮ ▮ L O V E S
S H A R I ▮ P R E S S ▮ I N A
E A R ▮ C A R E X H A U S T S
U N I S ▮ M I M E O ▮ R I I S
S E N T ▮ A Z U R E ▮ I N R E
E D G Y ▮ T E S T S ▮ S E E D
```

59

```
L O C H ▮ T A B O O ▮ J O B S
I N R E ▮ A S I A N ▮ E V E R
L E A P ▮ K I L T S ▮ R A R A
▮ A B C D E F G H I J K L M ▮
▮ ▮ A E C ▮ E S T A ▮ ▮ ▮
F A S T C A R ▮ E G R E S S
O S U ▮ R A N G ▮ G E N I E
L F I X L E V I R H Y O L D M
D I T K A ▮ E L I E ▮ A L I
S T E E L E ▮ N A S T I E S
▮ ▮ A N N S ▮ D E I ▮ ▮
▮ Z Y X W V U T S R Q P O N ▮
S I A M ▮ I R A T E ▮ O K E D
E T R E ▮ E S S E S ▮ F R A U
M I N N ▮ D E I S T ▮ F A T E
```

60

```
H E R E ▮ A C U T E ▮ G R O G
A M E S ▮ N O S I R ▮ L I M O
I M N O T G O I N G T O P A Y
G A T ▮ A L G A E ▮ A R E N A
▮ ▮ A S E A ▮ S U I ▮ ▮
S H O R T E N T H E P A N T S
T E S T Y ▮ H A R E ▮ O A K
R A C Y ▮ H B O M B ▮ T I K I
E V A ▮ D A R N ▮ P O S E R
W E R E I N A G R E E M E N T
▮ ▮ N A G ▮ E L S E ▮ ▮
F E I G N ▮ K A P U T ▮ I D A
I M S E E I N G A D O C T O R
F I L L ▮ N O R S E ▮ A C M E
I R E S ▮ S W A T S ▮ W H O A
```

Note: The answer to 39-Across, when translated by the cipher key at 20- and 55-Across (A=Z, B=Y, C=X, etc.), spells OUR COVER IS BLOWN.

61

```
S H A H   A W A K E   L I F T
H E D Y   R O S E S   O N E S
E M O P H I L I P S   C A S K
I M N O T A F A T A L I S T
L E A S T     A Y E   N I P
A R I   P O U L T   O L I V E
E S S O   A T E   E X E T E R
    B U T E V E N I F
O B S E S S   E L O   T A T I
V A N Y S   H E I S T   M O C
A D O   I W O     A P P L E
  O W E R E W H A T C O U L D
A D D S   I D O A B O U T I T
S E A T   S A B R A   R E N E
K A T E   S H O E R   S E G A
```

62

```
D E V O   C H E   A S S U R E
E L E V   O U I   S T A T E S
F O R E G O N E   T O R E A T
T I A R A   C I A   P A R L E
    W I T H O U T A H O M E
S H E E N S   T I T
R A D I O W A V E S   N I N A
A L I G N   D I U   C I N E S
S E T H   O V E R M O N T H S
    J O E   B R O L I N
L A R G E O R G I A N T
O T H E R   B I D   E C L A T
C R O O K S   D I D A H O R A
H I D D E N   D O A   K O O K
S P E E D O   Y T D   A N N E
```

63

```
A M E N   E S T E S   C A T S
S A L E   C H I M E   A M O I
S Y M B O L I C U N K N O W N
A B E R R A N T   E A R N S
M E R   D I S A S T E R
    A A F   C H A N D L E R
I R A N I   A T O M   O R O
R A T I N G F O R A D U L T S
A G T   R I E N   H A L E Y
Q U A G M I R E   M A W
    R E P E N T E R   U M P
P S H A W   D I A M E T E R
S I M P L E S I G N A T U R E
S L O E   P A N E L   T R I P
T O S S   A N G R Y   A N T S
```

64

```
A L S O   E S T A   E S S E N
L O I T E R E R S   E N U R E
A U R O R A A U S T R A L I S
S T E E R   L E N O   R T E S
    O A S   A R E A
  S I L L S   T A T I   N E E
A T N O   T O O T   L E A S T
R U S S I A N R O U L E T T E
T N U T S   T O I L   R E E S
S T L   E S O S   N O O S E
  A S E A   O A R
A L T E   L E N A   A L L I N
T R I N I T R O T O L U E N E
R O O S T   T E E N S I E S T
A N N E S   E L S E   S S T S
```

65

```
Z E T A   S O U S A   G R O W
H O O T   A N N U L   R A G E
O N T H E S T I C K   A I R E
U S H E R S   T R A M P L E D
    E I N E   S E L A H
T O P S I D E   I N S T E P
W R O T E   A G O N Y   H M O
I R I S   C R E P E   S E I S
N I N   M O N T E   B U L L S
E N T A I L   C H I N E S E
    P L U M A   E L B A
E X T R E M E S   A B O D E S
D R E I   B A C K T O W O R K
G A L L   U R I A H   L U G E
E Y E S   S A I L S   S T O W
```

66

```
A T L   H A S O N   R I C K S
T E A   O S T E O   E T A I L
D E T   W H E N P I G S F L Y
A T O M S   E N A M E L
W H Y Y O U L I T T L E
N E A L   N U N S     T E D
    O D I S T   S E A W A Y
W H E R E T H E B O Y S A R E
R U N D R Y   G L U E S
Y E S   I R E S   E M I T
    W H A T A W A Y T O G O
  I D I O T S   O S H E A
W H O L O V E S Y O U   A T T
O O Z E D   L A U E R   V I E
O P E D S   F O L D S   E T E
```

67

	S	H	O	R	T	I	E		A	S	K	E	R	S
I	C	E	B	O	A	T	S		V	I	N	N	I	E
B	A	L	L	Y	H	O	O		E	L	E	V	E	N
E	L	P	A	S	O			P	R	O	W	E	S	S
A	P	E	D		E	T	H	O	S		A	L	E	E
M	E	R	I	R		A	O	L		B	L	O	N	D
S	R	S		B	E	L	L	Y	F	L	O	P		
			B	I	L	L	Y	G	O	A	T			
		B	O	L	L	Y	W	O	O	D		L	E	T
A	G	I	R	L		H	A	N		E	P	O	D	E
L	O	G	E		M	O	R	S	E		I	N	I	T
A	T	T	I	R	E	S			L	E	N	G	T	H
R	H	I	N	O	S		B	U	L	L	Y	B	O	Y
M	I	M	O	S	A		A	T	E	L	I	E	R	S
S	C	E	N	E	S		R	E	S	A	N	D	S	

68

S	E	T	O	N		P	L	O	D		M	A	Z	E
P	R	O	V	O		E	E	K	A		U	R	I	S
L	A	Y	E	R		E	G	A	D		M	I	N	T
A	T	O	R		S	K	I	P	A	S	P	A	C	E
Y	O	U	R	I	N	I	T	I	A	L	S			
			A	T	E	N		S	R	O		S	I	B
T	S	E	T	S	E				T	W	E	N	T	Y
S	W	E	E	T		★	★	★		B	R	A	C	E
P	A	N	D	A	S				L	A	U	G	H	S
S	P	Y		K	I	A		S	O	L	D			
		P	E	R	S	O	N	A	L	I	Z	E	D	
M	Y	M	O	N	O	G	R	A	M		T	E	A	R
R	O	O	K		C	O	O	K		P	I	N	T	O
E	Y	R	E		C	O	N	E		M	O	D	U	S
D	O	E	R		O	D	O	R		S	N	A	P	S

★★★: Your initials

69

	T	O	T	A	L		B	O	L	T		D	E	W
C	A	P	I	T	A		A	P	S	E		A	M	E
H	I	T	M	E	N		D	E	A	N		T	A	N
O	P	I	E		A	G	E	N	T	A	G	E	N	T
R	E	N	T	S		A	G	A		M	I	D	A	S
D	I	G	I	T	D	I	G	I	T		N	A	T	O
			M	A	I	N		R	E	F		T	E	L
P	A	T	E	N	T				L	A	R	E	D	O
R	N	A		D	C	L		M	E	T	E			
A	N	K	A		H	E	L	I	X	H	E	L	I	X
N	O	E	L	S		D	E	S		A	D	O	R	E
D	U	T	C	H	D	U	T	C	H		R	U	I	N
I	N	A		O	O	P	S		U	S	E	D	T	O
A	C	K		A	N	T	I		R	E	E	L	I	N
L	E	E		L	E	O	N		L	A	D	Y	S	

70

S	T	I	C	K	S			W	I	S	T	E	R
T	E	N	O	N	E	D		E	L	P	A	S	O
I	N	S	P	I	R	I	T		B	L	I	M	P	S
F	L	A	T	F	I	S	H		P	O	K	E	R	S
L	E	N	I	E	N	C	E		A	M	E	L	I	E
E	Y	E	C	R	E	A	M		G	E	L	E	T	T
				R	I	F	E	N	E	S	S			
		P	R	O	M	D	R	E	S	S	E	S		
	P	R	O	P	O	S	A	L						
R	I	E	S	E	N		C	L	E	R	I	C	A	L
U	N	D	E	R	S		L	O	V	E	G	A	M	E
G	N	A	W	A	T		E	V	E	R	E	T	T	S
R	A	T	I	T	E		S	E	N	A	T	O	R	S
A	T	O	N	E	R		R	E	T	I	N	A	E	
T	E	R	E	S	A		R	E	T	A	K	E		

71

A	I	M	E	D		D	O	L	T		A	M	T	S
S	N	A	F	U		O	R	E	O		B	E	E	T
P	A	S	S	T	H	E	B	A	R		B	A	L	E
E	S	T		Y	E	S	I			S	A	L	L	E
N	E	E	R		N	O	T	B	A	D		T	A	P
S	C	R	A	M		K	E	E	P	S	T	I	L	L
			T	A	M		D	A	R		A	M	I	E
E	N	T	E	R	E	D		M	O	N	K	E	E	S
D	E	E	D		T	R	A		N	E	E			
H	A	N	G	T	O	U	G	H		V	O	C	A	L
A	R	T		R	O	M	E	O	S		N	O	M	E
R	E	A	D	Y		S	T	O	W		S	A	N	
R	A	C	E		G	R	A	B	S	O	M	E	Z	S
I	S	L	E		P	A	G	E		M	E	L	E	E
S	T	E	P		S	H	O	D		B	A	L	D	S

72

T	O	T	O		E	L	L	I	S		D	O	D	O
A	P	A	R		N	O	O	S	E		E	W	E	R
D	E	C	A		C	O	C	O	C	H	A	N	E	L
S	C	O	T	T	I	S	H			E	N	E	R	O
			I	O	N	E		R	A	P		D	E	N
Y	O	Y	O	C	O	N	T	E	S	T				
I	N	I	N	K		A	S	T	O		E	A	U	
P	U	P	S		M	A	N	T	A		E	M	I	R
E	S	S		K	O	N	G			E	Y	I	N	G
			N	O	N	O	N	A	N	E	T	T	E	
S	O	D		E	T	A		A	L	O	T			
A	R	E	N	A		O	M	E	L	E	T	T	E	
G	O	G	O	D	A	N	C	E	R		E	R	A	S
A	N	A	T		N	I	T	R	O		T	I	C	S
S	O	S	O		G	L	O	S	S		H	O	H	O

73

B	L	A	R	E		O	R	B	S		D	A	M	P
B	A	Y	E	D		R	E	E	K		E	S	A	U
C	I	N	C	I	N	N	A	T	I		S	T	I	R
		T	E	A	L		T	B	I	R	D	S		
A	L	S	O		A	T	I	T		A	R	O	S	E
P	E	E	R	P	R	E	S	S	U	R	E			
H	O	R	S	E		M	A	N	N		R	C	A	
I	N	F	O	R	C	E		R	O	O	T	O	U	T
D	E	S		S	Y	N	C		N	E	W	T	S	
			F	I	D	D	L	E	D	E	E	D	E	E
F	A	I	R	S		O	O	N	A		M	Y	R	A
I	N	N	A	T	E		S	T	U	N				
E	D	A	M		B	E	E	R	B	A	R	R	E	L
L	I	N	E		B	R	I	E		P	A	U	L	A
D	E	E	D		S	A	N	E		A	N	T	I	C

74

A	S	F	A	R	A	S		M	A	R	A	C	A	
M	A	R	S	A	L	A		A	D	A	M	A	N	T
A	G	A	K	H	A	N		S	A	N	T	A	N	A
N	A	N	A	S		D	R	A	M		S	N	A	P
A	S	S	N		B	A	L	S	A					
		T	A	M	A	R	A		B	A	N	N	S	
S	P	A		M	A	N	A		M	A	S	A	D	A
C	A	T	W	A	L	K		B	A	C	K	B	A	R
A	R	R	A	N	T		B	A	M	A		S	K	A
B	R	A	N	D		C	A	S	A	B	A			
		A	T	L	A	S		S	W	A	G			
G	A	L	A		H	A	S	P		P	L	A	T	H
A	L	A	S	K	A	N		A	T	L	A	N	T	A
G	A	S	T	A	N	K		R	W	A	N	D	A	N
	S	H	A	N	K	S		T	A	N	T	A	R	A

* The only vowel in the entire construction is A.

75

G	A	M		Ⓣ	S	O	I	L		Ⓣ	S	P	I	N
E	L	I		B	E	L	I	E		S	L	O	M	O
T	E	A		I	C	E	I	N		I	O	W	A	N
S	A	M	P	L	E		D	A	D	E				
Ⓛ	F	I	E	L	D	E	R		L	E	G	A	L	Ⓡ
		S	I	E	V	E		T	R	I	B	E	S	
E	G	G	O	N		E	S	T	O		N	O	T	I
Y	O	N		G	I	R	L	I	S	H		D	O	Z
E	T	A	L		S	I	A	M		I	R	E	N	E
S	T	R	A	F	E		T	E	S	T	Y			
Ⓛ	A	S	C	A	R		E	X	T	R	E	M	E	Ⓡ
		U	L	E	E		R	O	S	I	T	A		
S	A	E	N	S		M	U	S	I	C		L	A	W
U	L	N	A	E		I	N	I	N	K		E	P	A
B	E	L	L	Ⓑ		L	O	N	G	Ⓑ		R	E	Y

Ⓣ = Top, Ⓑ = Bottom
Ⓛ = Left, Ⓡ = Right

Solution to the teaser puzzle from
The New York Times Crossword All-Stars

R	I	B	S		A	V	I	A	S		A	M	M	O
O	M	O	O		R	I	N	G	O		R	A	I	N
Y	O	U	R	P	L	A	C	E	O	R	M	I	N	E
A	N	N	E	H	E	C	H	E		E	E	N		
L	I	C		I	S	O		S	L	E	D	G	E	
S	T	E	T		M	A	T	T	E		R	U	M	
		R	A	E		P	H	E	A	S	A	N	T	
	W	H	A	T	S	Y	O	U	R	S	I	G	N	
D	I	A	M	E	T	E	R		N	E	T			
A	N	Y		C	E	N	T	S		S	H	E	A	
R	E	F	E	R	S		E	P	A		I	T	S	
	E	X	O		A	R	E	A	C	O	D	E	S	
H	A	V	E	W	E	M	E	T	B	E	F	O	R	E
E	W	E	R		L	E	A	H	S		F	U	N	T
P	E	R	T		I	N	L	E	T		S	T	E	S

The New York Times
Crossword Puzzles

The #1 name in crosswords

Millions of fans know that *New York Times* crosswords are the pinnacle of puzzledom. Challenge your brain with these quality titles from St. Martin's Griffin.

Available at your local bookstore or online at nytimes.com/nystore

Coming Soon

Crossword All-Stars	0-312-31004-8	$9.95/$14.95 Can.
Crosswords for the Work Week	0-312-30952-X	$6.95/$9.95 Can.
Bonus Crosswords	0-312-31003-X	$9.95/$14.95 Can.
Sunday Omnibus Vol. 7	0-312-30950-3	$12.95/$18.95 Can.
Daily Vol. 63	0-312-30947-3	$9.95/$14.95 Can.

Daily Crosswords

Monday through Friday	0-312-30058-1	$9.95/$14.95 Can.
Daily Crosswords Vol. 62	0-312-30512-5	$9.95/$14.95 Can.
Daily Crosswords Vol. 61	0-312-30057-3	$9.95/$14.95 Can.
Daily Crosswords Vol. 60	0-312-28977-2	$9.95/$14.95 Can.
Daily Crosswords Vol. 59	0-312-28413-6	$9.95/$14.95 Can.
Daily Crosswords Vol. 58	0-312-28171-4	$9.95/$14.95 Can.
Daily Crosswords Vol. 57	0-312-28170-6	$9.95/$14.95 Can.

Easy Crosswords

Easy Crosswords Vol. 3	0-312-28912-X	$9.95/$14.95 Can.
Easy Crosswords Vol. 2	0-312-28172-2	$9.95/$14.95 Can.

Tough Crosswords

Tough Crosswords Vol. 10	0-312-30060-3	$10.95/$15.95 Can.
Tough Crosswords Vol. 9	0-312-28173-0	$10.95/$15.95 Can.

Sunday Crosswords

Sunday Crosswords Vol. 28	0-312-30515-X	$9.95/$14.95 Can.
Sunday Crosswords Vol. 27	0-312-28414-4	$9.95/$14.95 Can.

Large Print Crosswords

Large Print Crossword Omnibus Vol. 4	0-312-30514-1	$12.95/$18.95 Can.

Large Print Crosswords (continued)

Large Print Crossword Omnibus Vol. 3	0-312-28841-1	$12.95/$18.95 Can.

Omnibus

Easy Omnibus Vol. 1	0-312-30513-3	$11.95/$17.95 Can.
Daily Omnibus Vol. 12	0-312-30511-7	$11.95/$17.95 Can.
Daily Omnibus Vol. 11	0-312-28412-8	$11.95/$17.95 Can.
Sunday Omnibus Vol. 6	0-312-28913-8	$11.95/$17.95 Can.

Variety Puzzles

Acrostic Crosswords Vol. 8	0-312-28410-1	$9.95/$14.95 Can.
Sunday Variety Puzzles	0-312-30059-X	$9.95/$14.95 Can.

Portable Size Format

Super Saturday	0-312-30604-0	$6.95/$9.95 Can.
Crosswords for the Holidays	0-312-30603-2	$6.95/$9.95 Can.
Sun, Sand, and Crosswords	0-312-30076-X	$6.95/$9.95 Can.
Weekend Challenge	0-312-30079-4	$6.95/$9.95 Can.
Crosswords for Your Coffee Break	0-312-28830-1	$6.95/$9.95 Can.

For Young Solvers

New York Times on the Web Crosswords for Teens	0-312-28911-1	$6.95/$9.95 Can.
Outrageous Crossword PUzzles and Word Games for Kids	0-312-28915-4	$6.95/$9.95 Can.
More Outrageous Crossword Puzzles and Word Games for Kids	0-312-30062-X	$6.95/$9.95 Can.

Sign up today for crossword puzzle news, contests, and updates by e-mailing crosswords@stmartins.com!

ST. MARTIN'S GRIFFIN